Collins

Mission:
français

Workbook 1

Oliver Gray

Series Editor: Linzy Dickinson

William Collins's dream of knowledge for all began with the publication of his first book in 1819. A self-educated mill worker, he not only enriched millions of lives, but also founded a flourishing publishing house. Today, staying true to this spirit, Collins books are packed with inspiration, innovation and practical expertise. They place you at the centre of a world of possibility and give you exactly what you need to explore it.

Collins. Freedom to teach.

Published by Collins
An imprint of HarperCollins*Publishers*
77–85 Fulham Palace Road
Hammersmith
London
W6 8JB

Browse the complete Collins catalogue at
www.harpercollins.co.uk

ISBN-13 978-0-00-751344-4

British Library Cataloguing in Publication Data
A Catalogue record for this publication is available from the British Library.

Commissioned by Katie Sergeant
Series concept by Linzy Dickinson
Project managed by Elektra Media Ltd
Development edited by Naomi Laredo
Copy-edited by Claire Trocmé
Concept design by Elektra Media Ltd
Illustrations by Elektra Media Ltd
Typeset by Jouve India Private Limited
Cover design by Angela English

Printed and bound by L.E.G.O. S.p.A. Italy

Acknowledgements
The publishers wish to thank the following for permission to reproduce photographs. Every effort has been made to trace copyright holders and to obtain their permission for the use of copyright materials. The publishers will gladly receive any information enabling them to rectify any error or omission at the first opportunity.

(t = top, c = centre, b = bottom, r = right, l = left)

Cover tl prochasson Frederic/Shutterstock, cover tr haraldmuc/Shutterstock, cover br Kirsz Marcin/Shutterstock, cover bl Roman Sigaev/Shutterstock, p 10 Fotosports/Photoshot, p 23tl Albert Barr/iStockphoto, p 23tr Cristian Lazzari/iStockphoto, p 23 ctl Christophe Testi/iStockphoto, p 23ctr Mikhail Zahranichny/Shutterstock, p 23cbl stockcam/iStockphoto, p 23cbr vvoe/Shutterstock, p 23bl Retna/Photoshot, p 23br Jean-Yves Benedeyt/iStockphoto, p 26 EdStock/iStockphoto, p 61tl kodachrome25/iStockphoto, p 61tr tompozzo/iStockphoto, p 61bl Bareta/iStockphoto, p 61br Anze Mulec/Shutterstock, p 63t Puy du Fou, p 63ct Barbara Boensch/image/imagebroker.net/SuperStock, p 63c *VolcanBul* Camus-Vulcania, p 63cb Les Editions Albert René/Goscinny-Uderzo/S.Cambon, p 63b glen gaffney/Shutterstock, p 74l PRILL/Shutterstock, p 74r Mstyslav Chernov/Shutterstock, p 83 Claudio Giovanni Colombo/Shutterstock, p 91t velirina/Shutterstock, p 91b Jorge Felix Costa/Shutterstock.

Mon autoportrait

Draw your self-portrait and complete the sentences below.

Je m'appelle _____ .

Ma classe est _____ .

Tableau des contenus

Module 4 Escapades

Module 5 Espace culturel

Notes

- Pupil Book pages 8–9

Aujourd'hui, c'est le _____ . Il est _____ .

Langue et grammaire

Asking someone how they are

Here are three ways of asking this question:

Ça va?	To use with a friend or someone you know very well
Comment ça va?	To use with a young person you don't know well
Comment allez-vous?	To use with an adult who isn't a close friend

Using verbs (doing words)

Learning to use French verbs is very important. Regular verbs follow patterns you can learn to use. Those that don't follow these patterns are called irregular verbs.

To talk about how you are feeling you can use the verb *être* (to be). It's an irregular verb.

Look at how it works:

je suis	I am	*tu es*	you are
il est	he is	*elle est*	she is

Using adjectives (describing words)

In French, the spelling of an adjective often changes depending on the person or thing it is describing. For example, many have an extra 'e' at the end to show that they are describing a girl or woman.

Pronunciation

The cedilla mark under the letter 'c' (ç) before the letters 'a', 'o' and 'u' makes it sound like the letter 's'. The letter 'c' always sounds like the letter 's' in front of the letters 'e' and 'i'.
Listen to the sound of the letter é, for example in the word *fatigué*.

 1 What would you say? Underline the correct expression.

   a To your doctor: Ça va? / Comment ça va? / <u>Comment allez-vous?</u>

   b To a close friend: Ça va? / Comment ça va? / Comment allez-vous?

   c To your teacher: Ça va? / Comment ça va? / Comment allez-vous?

   d To someone you know quite well: Ça va? / Comment ça va? / Comment allez-vous?

2 Practise out loud. Ask these people how they are.

   a an adult neighbour   <u>Comment allez-vous?</u>

   b your brother   _____

   c your best friend   _____

   d a girl you've met before _____

   e the postman   _____

3 Draw lines to link the French expressions to the pictures.

1 Ça va bien, merci.

2 Ça va très mal aujourd'hui.

3 Comme ci comme ça.

4 Bof! Pas mal.

5 Ça va super bien.

a

b

c

d

e

4 Fill in the gaps in the conversation with words from the list.

| suis | ~~va~~ | ça | très | toi | que |

Salut, Paul. Ça ___va___ ?

Ça va bien, merci, Amina! Et _____?

_____ va _____ mal aujourd'hui.

Ah bon, pourquoi?

Parce _____ je _____ fatiguée.

5 Write down how these people feel.

a Chloé only got two hours' sleep last night. *Chloé est* fatiguée _____.

b Louis has got a rotten cold. *Louis est* m_____.

c Sarah has had some bad news. *Sarah est* t_____.

d Everything has gone wrong today for Emma. *Emma est* s_____.

e Hugo didn't get to bed till very late. *Hugo est* f_____.

f Maëlle has toothache. *Maëlle est* m_____.

6 Translate these words into English.

a French: merci   English: _____

b French: pourquoi?   English: _____

c French: très   English: _____

d French: et toi?   English: _____

e French: pas mal   English: _____

f French: parce que   English: _____

7 Are these statements true or false? ⭐

Bonjour. Ça va? Moi, je suis Estelle. Aujourd'hui, ça va mal. Je suis fatiguée et je suis stressée. Pourquoi? Parce que je suis malade.

a Estelle is talking.   _____True_____

b Estelle is ill.   _____

c She's feeling happy.   _____

d She's stressed out.   _____

e She isn't tired.   _____

f She asks how you are.   _____

8 Say how you're feeling in French. ⭐

a You're feeling great.   _____Ça va super bien._____

b You're feeling bad.   _____

c You're feeling good.   _____

d You're feeling sad.   _____

e You're feeling stressed.   _____

• Pupil Book pages 10–11

Aujourd'hui, c'est le _____ . Il est _____ .

Langue et grammaire

Using the verb *être*
You learned how to say 'I am' using the verb *être* in the previous topic. Here is a reminder of the other forms of the same verb that you looked at:

je suis	I am	*tu es*	you are	
il est	he is	*elle est*	she is	

Making a negative sentence
Use *ne* and *pas* around a verb to make it negative. For example:

Je suis timide.	I'm shy.
*Je **ne** suis **pas** timide.*	I'm not shy.
Il est drôle.	He's funny.
*Il **n'**est **pas** drôle.*	He isn't funny.
Elle est sympa.	She's friendly.
*Elle **n'**est **pas** sympa.*	She isn't friendly.

Notice how 'ne' changes to 'n' when the verb starts with a vowel.

Asking what someone is like
Ask:

Tu es comment?	What are you like?
Il/Elle est comment?	What is he/she like?

Remember, your voice must go up to sound like a question.

Pronunciation
If a word in French ends in a 't', 's' or 'd', you don't pronounce the last letter. For example:
bavard, intelligent
If a word ends in 'te' or 'de' then you do pronounce the 't' or 'd'. For example, *intelligen**te**, bavar**de***.

---

1 Draw lines to link the French and English expressions.

pas du tout	false
un peu	also
assez	very
mais	true
aussi	quite
vrai	a bit
faux	too
très	but
trop	not at all

2 Copy a French word from the box below to describe these people.

| sympa | intelligente | timide | paresseux | drôle | impatiente | bavarde |

a Maeva never stops talking. _____bavarde_____

b Sophie gets annoyed when the bus is late. _____

c Justine always gets top marks at school. _____

d Abdou blushes when meeting new people. _____

e Lucas lies around on the sofa all day. _____

f Félix is a great laugh. _____

g Everyone likes Manon. _____

3 Unjumble these anagrams of French adjectives.

a metidi _____timide_____

b eliaroansnb _____

c rabvda _____

d xarsepesu _____

e miptienat _____

f yaspm _____

g ntleineitlg _____

4 Write *M* if the word describes a male person and *F* if the person is female. (One word could be either, so put *M/F*.)

a bavard _____M_____

b paresseuse _____

c bavarde _____

d impatient _____

e intelligente _____

f paresseux _____

g sympa _____

h intelligent _____

5 Circle the correct answer according to the text.

Voici Thierry. Thierry est très sympa et assez drôle. Il n'est pas paresseux et il n'est pas timide. Thierry est assez intelligent et aussi un peu bavard.

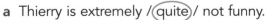

a Thierry is extremely /(quite)/ not funny.

d He is / isn't lazy.

c He's quite / very / not intelligent.

f He's not / quite / very friendly.

e He is extremely / a bit / not chatty.

b He is / isn't shy.

6 Write in *suis* or *est*.

a Je _suis_ paresseux.

b Elle _____ timide.

c Il _____ intelligent.

d Je _____ bavarde.

e Je _____ impatient.

f Elle _____ drôle.

7 Write a few lines about yourself. Copy this outline and fill in the gaps. It doesn't all have to be true!

Bonjour! Je m'appelle _____. Je pense que je suis très _____ et _____. Je ne suis pas du tout _____, mais je suis assez _____. Je suis trop _____.

Need more adjectives? Ask your teacher or use a dictionary.

_____

_____

_____

_____

8 Now choose someone else. It can be a famous person or a friend. Use the outline from exercise 7 but replace *je* with *il* or *elle* and *suis* with *est*. Remember, if your subject is not the same gender as you, some adjectives may change. ⭐

_____

_____

_____

_____

• Pupil Book pages 12–13

Aujourd'hui, c'est le _____ . Il est 🕐 _____ .

Langue et grammaire

Describing people

To describe someone's height and build, use the verb *être*. You have seen this in the last two topics:

je suis petit   I am small
je ne suis pas grand   I am not tall

Use the verb *avoir* to talk about the kind of hair and eyes someone has. Look at how this verb works:

j'ai   I have
tu as   you have
il a   he has
elle a   she has

Using adjectives correctly

You've already seen how an adjective can change depending on whether it is describing a male or female person. An adjective also changes if it is describing more than one thing or more than one person. For example, the words for eyes and hair are both plural so you add an 's' to adjectives you use to describe them:

les yeux bleus   blue eyes
les cheveux blonds   blond hair

The adjective *marron* is unusual and does **not** change:

les yeux marron   brown eyes

Adjectives usually go after the noun they are describing. Look at the examples above again.

Pronunciation

The letter 'x' at the end of a word is silent: *cheveux, yeux*
The letter combination *aille* is pronounced like the English word 'eye': *de taille moyenne*.

 1   Who is being described? Underline Nathan or Marielle.

   Nathan   Marielle

a <u>Nathan</u> / Marielle a les cheveux bruns.

b Nathan / Marielle a les cheveux blonds.

c Nathan / Marielle a les yeux bleus.

d Nathan / Marielle a les cheveux courts.

e Nathan / Marielle a les cheveux longs.

f Nathan / Marielle a les yeux marron.

2 Now describe your own eyes and hair. Fill in the gaps.

J'ai les yeux _____ et les cheveux _____ et _____.

3 Play a guessing game in pairs. You describe one of your classmates and your partner guesses who you are talking about. Then swap roles.

Il/Elle a les yeux _____ et les cheveux _____ et _____.

4 Draw lines to link the French and English expressions.

she is	j'ai
he has	tu es
I am	elle est
I have	il est
you are	tu as
she has	je suis
he is	il a
you have	elle a

5 Write *M* if the adjective describes a male person and *F* if the person is female. If it could be either, put *M/F*.

a grand   M

b petite   _____

c mince   _____

d petit   _____

e grande   _____

f grosse   _____

g gros   _____

6 Write in the missing adjectives. Remember to use the correct form (masculine or feminine).

a Marine n'est pas mince.   Elle est ____grosse____.

b Robert n'est pas grand.   Il est _____.

c Nathan n'est pas petit.   Il est _____.

d Yasmine n'est pas grosse.   Elle est _____.

e Amir n'est pas mince.   Il est _____.

f Sofia n'est pas petite.   Elle est _____.

7 Translate these sentences into English. ⭐

a Il n'est pas gros.   ____He isn't fat.____

b Elle est de taille moyenne.   _____

c Elle n'est pas grande.   _____

d Il n'est pas petit.   _____

e Elle a les cheveux bruns.   _____

f Elle a les cheveux mi-longs.   _____

g Il est grand mais il n'est pas gros.   _____

h Elle est grande et elle est mince aussi.   _____

8 Translate these sentences into French. ⭐

a He isn't fat.   ____Il n'est pas gros.____

b She isn't tall.   _____

c He is short and thin.   _____

d He has red hair.   _____

e She has green eyes.   _____

f She is of medium build.   _____

Topic 4 La famille type

- Pupil Book pages 14–15

 Aujourd'hui, c'est le _____. Il est _____.

Langue et grammaire

Using masculine and feminine nouns

Nouns in French are masculine or feminine. Use *un* to mean 'a' for a masculine noun and *une* to mean 'a' for a feminine noun:

un frère   a brother   *une sœur*   a sister

Making a noun plural

In most cases, add 's' just like in English:

J'ai deux frères.   I have two brothers.
J'ai trois sœurs.   I have three sisters.

Talking about age

Use the verb *avoir* to talk about age. You learned how to use *avoir* in the previous topic.

J'ai douze ans.   I'm twelve years old.
Tu as quel âge?   How old are you?
Il/elle a seize ans.   He/she is sixteen years old.

Using 'my' and your'

There are three French words for 'my' and three for 'your'. To know which word to use, check whether the noun that comes after it is masculine, feminine or plural.

	masculine	feminine	plural
my	mon	ma	mes
your	ton	ta	tes

For example:

mon frère	my brother	*ton frère*	your brother
ma sœur	my sister	*ta sœur*	your sister
mes frères	my brothers	*tes sœurs*	your sisters

Pronunciation

If a word ending in 's' or 'x' is followed by a word beginning with a vowel, you pronounce the 's' or 'x', although usually it is silent. For example: *trois ans*

---

1 How old are these people? Write in their ages.

a J'ai douze ans.   12   **b** J'ai treize ans.   _____

c J'ai onze ans.   _____   **d** J'ai quatorze ans.   _____

e J'ai vingt ans.   _____   **f** J'ai dix-huit ans.   _____

g J'ai seize ans.   _____   **h** J'ai quinze ans.   _____

2 Read aloud what the people in exercise 1 are saying. Say your own age as well. Then ask a few people *Tu as quel âge?* and note down their answers.

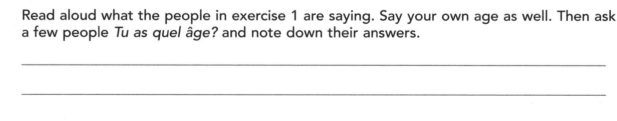

_____

_____

_____

3 Write in the numbers in French.

3   4   7   8   10

trois   _____   _____   _____

12   15   17   19   20

_____   _____   _____   _____   _____

4 Who is speaking? Write in a name.

Nathan   **Fatima**   **Chloé**   **Charlie**   **Marielle**

a J'ai un frère et une sœur.   Chloé _____

b Je suis fille unique.   _____

c Je suis fils unique.   _____

d J'ai une grande famille.   _____

e J'ai deux sœurs.   _____

5 Draw lines to link the French and English expressions.

mon frère   your brothers

ta sœur   your brother

mes sœurs   my brother

ma sœur   my sisters

ton frère   your sister

mes frères   my brothers

tes frères   your sisters

tes sœurs   my sister

6 Write in *mon, ma, mes, ton, ta* or *tes.*

a   __mon__   frère (my)

b _____ sœurs (your)

c _____ sœur (my)

d _____ frères (your)

e _____ sœur (your)

f _____ frère (your)

7 Read Mehdi's description and fill in the information below. ⭐

Salut! Je m'appelle Mehdi et j'ai douze ans. J'ai une grande famille. J'ai deux frères et une soeur. Mon petit frère s'appelle Noam et il a trois ans. Mon grand frère s'appelle Amir et il a quinze ans. Ma soeur s'appelle Maya et elle a cinq ans.

Name: *Mehdi*

Little brother's name: _____

Little brother's age: _____

Older brother's name: _____

Older brother's age: _____

Sister's name: _____

Sister's age: _____

8 Now write a similar paragraph for this person. ⭐

I D

NAME:	**Marine**
AGE:	**11 ans**
YOUNGER SISTER:	**Olivia, 8 ans**
OLDER SISTER:	**Anne, 16 ans**
YOUNGER BROTHER:	**Lucas, 6 ans**

_____

_____

_____

_____

• Pupil Book pages 16–17

Aujourd'hui, c'est le _____ . Il est _____ .

Langue et grammaire

Using verbs

Verbs are used to talk about what people do. In French, the most common type of verbs are –er verbs, like *habiter* (to live) and *parler* (to speak):

parler	to speak	*habiter*	to live
je parle	I speak	*j'habite*	I live
tu parles	you speak	*tu habites*	you live
il/elle parle	he/she speaks	*il/elle habite*	he/she lives

Notice how *je* changes in *j'habite*. You've seen this before with *j'ai* (I have). This is because the letter 'h' in French is silent.

Using nouns

All nouns in French are either masculine or feminine, not just the ones to do with people. Remember to use *le* (the) or *un* (a/an) with a masculine noun and *la* (the) or *une* (a/an) with a feminine noun.

Questions

The French word *où* means 'where'. If you write *ou* without the accent, it sounds the same but it means 'or', so make sure you remember the accent!

To ask someone where they live:
Tu habites où?

1 Read the text and fill in the gaps in the sentences in English.

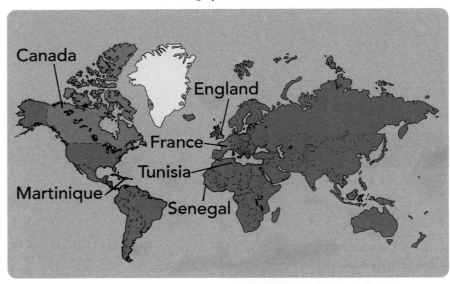

Samil habite au Sénégal, Pierre habite en France, Oliver habite en Angleterre, Sophie habite au Canada, Thérèse habite en Tunisie et Kenzo habite en Martinique.

a Thérèse lives in ___Tunisia___ . **b** Samil lives in _____ .

c Sophie lives in _____ . **d** Oliver lives in _____ .

e Kenzo lives in _____ . **f** Pierre lives in _____ .

2 Complete the sentences with *en, au* or *à la*.

a Pierre habite ___en___ France.

b Sophie habite _____ Canada.

c Kenzo habite _____ Martinique.

d Samil habite _____ Sénégal.

e Oliver habite _____ Angleterre.

f Thérèse habite _____ Tunisie.

3 **a** Ask a few classmates where they live: *Tu habites où?* Make sure they reply giving both the country and the town, for example: *J'habite en Angleterre, à Bristol.*

b Answer the question your classmates ask you.

4 Some of these verbs need an *–s* on the end. Add it where it's necessary. Draw a dash (–) if it isn't.

a J'habite _–_ en France.

b Tu parle___ français?

c Il parle___ arabe.

d Tu t'appelle___ comment?

e Tu habite___ où?

f Elle habite___ au Canada.

g Elle s'appelle___ Agnés.

h Il parle___ créole.

5 Write *Je* or *J'* in front of these verbs.

a _Je_ m'appelle

b _____ habite

c _____ parle

d _____ suis

e _____ ai

6 Who is saying these things? Circle boy or girl.

a Je suis anglais. (boy) / girl

b Je suis canadienne. boy / girl

c Je suis française. boy / girl

d Je suis sénégalais. boy / girl

e Je suis tunisienne. boy / girl

f Je suis canadien. boy / girl

7 Give these people's nationality in French.

a Elle est sénégalaise.

b _____

c _____

d _____

e _____

a   b

c   d   e

8 Read this information and answer the questions in English. ⭐

> Salut! Je m'appelle Émilie et j'habite à Montréal, au Canada. Je suis canadienne et je parle anglais et français parce qu'on parle deux langues au Canada. Mon père est canadien mais ma mère est anglaise.

a What nationality is Émilie?   Canadian

b What nationality is her mother?   _____

c What nationality is her father?   _____

d Which languages does she speak?   _____

e Which city does she live in?   _____

9 Now write a similar paragraph about yourself. ⭐

Mention:

- the town where you live
- which country it is in
- your nationality
- your parents' nationality/nationalities
- which languages you speak

_____

_____

_____

_____

Topic 6 Un portrait de ma ville

• Pupil Book pages 18–19

Aujourd'hui, c'est le _____ . Il est _____ .

Langue et grammaire

Il y a

You can use the phrase *il y a* to talk about what there is in a place. This phrase can mean both 'there is' and 'there are' so it is very useful. For example: *Qu'est-ce qu'il y a à Paris? Il y a des monuments. Il n'y a pas de volcan!*

What is there in Paris? There are monuments. There is no volcano!

Notice that *il n'y a pas* is always followed by *de*, instead of *un*, *une* or *des*.

Using nouns

You've already seen how to use *un* and *une* when talking about one item. To talk about more than one item, use *des*, which means 'some'.
Look at these examples:

un magasin	a shop
des magasins	some shops
une plage	a beach
des plages	some beaches

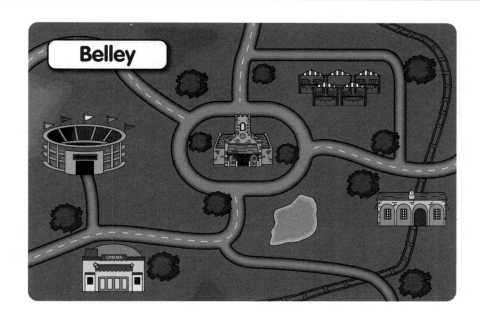

Belley

 Answer the questions with *oui* or *non*.

a Est-ce qu'il y a un stade? ____oui____   b Est-ce qu'il y a un port? _____

c Est-ce qu'il y a une église? _____   d Est-ce qu'il y a un marché? _____

e Est-ce qu'il y a une plage? _____   f Est-ce qu'il y a une gare? _____

g Est-ce qu'il y a un cinéma? _____   h Est-ce qu'il y a une patinoire? _____

2 Now write five true French sentences about Belley.

a Il y a _____une gare_____ .

b Il y a _____ .

c Il y a _____ .

d Il y a _____ .

e Il y a _____ .

3 Write *un* or *une* in front of these words.

a __une__ bibliothèque

b _____ village

c _____ ville

d _____ gare

e _____ magasin

f _____ centre commercial

g _____ port

h _____ plage

4 Draw lines to link the French and English expressions.

some shops

a church

some churches

a shop

a beach

some cinemas

some beaches

a cinema

une église

des cinémas

une plage

des plages

un cinéma

un magasin

des églises

des magasins

5 Translate these phrases into English.

a des églises   _____some churches_____

b il y a   _____

c un magasin   _____

d il n'y a pas   _____

e une bibliothèque   _____

f des magasins   _____

6 Next to these words, write M for masculine or F for feminine.

a une ferme ___F___ b un volcan _____

c un stade _____ d une tante _____

e un oncle _____ f un marché _____

g une patinoire _____ h une église _____

7 Contradict these sentences (write the opposite). ⭐

a Il y a un centre commercial.   _____Non. Il n'y a pas de centre commercial._____

b Il y a une ferme.   _____

c Il y a un magasin.   _____

d Il y a un volcan.   _____

8 Describe these pictures. Follow the example. ⭐

a

_____Il y a une église mais il n'y a pas de musée._____

b

_____

c

_____

d

_____

9 Invent a town and write a description of it in French. ⭐

_____

_____

_____

• Pupil Book pages 32–33

Aujourd'hui, c'est le [calendar] _____ . Il est [clock] _____ .

Langue et grammaire

Asking what something is like
To ask what something is like, say:
C'est comment?   What's it like?
Remember to lift your voice at the end.

Using verbs
You've already seen some regular *–er* verbs in Module 1. In this topic you'll see several more of these. Remember, this is the pattern they follow:

manger	to eat
je mange	I eat
tu manges	you eat
il mange	he eats
elle mange	she eats
on mange	we eat

Using *on*
On is a fairly informal way of saying 'we' in French and is used a lot. Look at the verb *manger* above and notice how the form of verb used with *on* is the same as the form used for *il* or *elle*.

Pronunciation
Remember not to pronounce the 's' at the end of the *tu* form of the verbs. An 's' at the end of a word is not usually pronounced in French.

Write in the French words, one letter per box. Find the word in the tinted boxes (reading downwards) and translate it into English.

1 kitchen: `c` `u` `i` `▓` ` ` ` ` ` `

2 dining room: ` ` ` ` ` ` ` ` ` `   ` `   ` ` `▓` ` ` ` ` ` ` ` `

3 bathroom: ` ` ` ` ` ` `▓` ` `   ` ` ` `   ` ` ` ` ` ` ` ` `

4 house: ` ` ` ` ` ` `▓` ` `

5 garden: ` ` ` ` ` ` ` ` `▓`

Solution: _____ = _____

2 These children are playing hide and seek. Write down, in English, where they are.

a Je suis dans la salle de bains. _____bathroom_____

b Je suis dans le jardin. _____

c Je suis dans le salon. _____

d Je suis dans la salle à manger _____

e Je suis dans la cuisine. _____

f Je suis dans la chambre. _____

3 Work in pairs. A thinks of a place to hide. B guesses where he or she is. If B doesn't get it in three guesses, they've lost. Then swap roles.

Exemple

A Tu es dans la cuisine?

B Non!

4 Circle the correct words.

a J'(habite)/ habites dans un appartement.　　b On mange / manges dans la cuisine.

c Elle chantes / chante dans un groupe.　　d Tu écoute / écoutes de la musique.

e Je partages / partage ma chambre.　　f On regarde / regardes la télé le soir.

g Il joues / joue aux cartes.　　h Tu habite / habites où?

5 Translate all the sentences in exercise 4 into English.

a I live in a flat. _____

b _____

c _____

d _____

e _____

f _____

g _____

h _____

6   Unjumble the sentences and write them out correctly.

a Dans petit J' un appartement habite

J'habite dans un petit appartement.

b On dans maison habite grande une

_____

c habite appartement Elle grand un dans

_____

d maison petite habites Tu une dans

_____

7   Read what Rémi says. Are the sentences true or false? ☆

J'habite à Guadeloupe dans une grande maison avec ma mère, mon père et mon petit frère Noé. Chez moi, il y a une grande cuisine. On mange dans la salle à manger. Il y a trois chambres et une salle de bains – naturellement. On joue au foot dans le jardin. Ici il fait beau tous les jours.

a Rémi is an only child.   _____false_____

b His house is big.   _____

c His parents are divorced.   _____

d They eat in the kitchen.   _____

e They don't have a dining room.   _____

f There is only one bathroom.   _____

g They play football in the garden.   _____

h It rains a lot in Guadeloupe.   _____

8   Now write a description of your own house or flat. Mention all the rooms and what you do in them. Try to use the *on* form and *il y a*. Write at least six lines. ☆

_____

_____

_____

_____

_____

_____

- Pupil Book pages 34–35

Aujourd'hui, c'est le _____ . Il est _____ .

Langue et grammaire

Using prepositions

Prepositions are used to talk about where things are. They're easy to use.

Dans ma chambre...	In my bedroom...
Ma guitare est sous le lit.	My guitar is under the bed.
Ma guitare est sur le lit.	My guitar is on the bed.
Ma guitare est derrière la porte.	My guitar is behind the door.

The indefinite article and the definite article

The indefinite article in English is 'a' or 'an'. In French, use:

un for a masculine noun	*un lit*	a bed
une for a feminine noun	*une porte*	a door
des for a plural noun	*des étagères*	some shelves

The definite article in English is 'the'. In French, use:

le for a masculine noun	*le lit*	the bed
la for a feminine noun	*la porte*	the door
les for a plural noun	*les lits*	the beds

Pronunciation

Practise how to pronounce *sur* and *sous* so you don't get them mixed up. Push your lips forward into a pout for *sous*.

Notice how words ending in *–able* are pronounced differently in French. For example, *un portable*. Accents change the pronunciation of the letter 'e'. Listen carefully to the word *étagère*. What other words do you know containing é or è?

 1 Put *un* or *une* in front of each word. Then draw a line to link each word to its picture.

a ___une___ guitare

b _____ portefeuille

c _____ ballon de basket

d _____ montre

e _____ trottinette

f _____ portable

2 Look at these words Decide what gender they are. Write in *le* or *la* or *l'* and *un* or *une*.

Definite article	Indefinite article
_le_ lit	_un_ lit
____ étagère	____ étagère
____ tapis	____ tapis
____ table	____ table
____ pouf-poire	____ pouf-poire
____ porte	____ porte

3 Work in pairs. Think of a place to hide something in your room. Write it down. Your partner has to guess where it is, using *sur*, *sous*, *dans* or *derrière*. Then swap roles.

Exemple
A Il/elle est derrière l'étagère?
B Non!

4 Unjumble these anagrams of adjectives.

a loco _____ _cool_ _____

b raqpiteu _____

c atmasun _____

d oenrmed _____

5 Look at the picture and complete the sentences with *sur*, *sous*, *dans* or *derrière*.

a Le portefeuille est __sur__ le lit.

b Le portable est _____ l'étagère.

c La trottinette est _____ la porte.

d La montre est _____ le tapis.

e Le ballon de basket est _____ la table.

f La guitare est _____ le pouf-poire.

6 Read the text and answer the questions.

a Does Simon like his room?

_yes_____

b Why?

_____

c Which does he like more: his bed or his guitar?

_____

d What does he think of his basketball?

_____

e What does he not like?

_____

f Why?

_____

Simon

J'adore ma chambre parce qu'elle est cool. J'aime mon lit parce qu'il est pratique et confortable. J'adore ma guitare parce qu'elle est moderne et j'aime mon ballon de basket parce qu'il est amusant. Mais je n'aime pas mon tapis parce qu'il est vert!

7 Translate into English: ⭐

a Mon portable est moderne.
b Mon portefeuille est pratique.
c Dans ma chambre, j'ai un lit.
d Ma montre est sur l'étagère.
e J'adore ma chambre.
f Je n'aime pas mon tapis.

_My mobile phone is_____

_____

_____

_____

_____

_____

8 Translate into French: ⭐

a on the table
b I love my mobile phone.
c My watch is cool.
d I have a bed.
e because it's modern
f There is a door.

_sur la table_____

_____

_____

_____

_____

_____

- Pupil Book pages 36–37

Aujourd'hui, c'est le _____ . Il est 🕐 _____ .

Langue et grammaire

Telling the time

To say what time it is, use the phrase *Il est...*

Il est cinq heures.	It's five o'clock.
Il est deux heures dix.	It's ten past two.
Il est huit heures moins cinq.	It's five to eight.
Il est cinq heures et quart.	It's quarter past five.
Il est neuf heures moins le quart.	It's quarter to nine.
Il est deux heures et demie.	It's half past two.

When it's one o'clock, the word *heure* is singular so it is spelled without an 's'.
Il est une heure.

The 24-hour clock is very often used in France and around the world:

Il est dix heures.	It's 10 a.m.
Il est quinze heures.	It's 3 p.m.

If you want to use the 12-hour clock in French, use the phrases *du matin* and *du soir*:

Il est huit heures du matin.	It's eight o'clock in the morning.
Il est neuf heures du soir.	It's nine o'clock in the evening.

Questions

The word *quel(le)* is used to ask 'what' or 'which'. When you ask a question using *quel(le)*, you swap the positions of the subject and the verb, like this:

Quelle heure est-il?	What time is it?

Notice the hyphen in *est-il*.

Pronunciation

In French, the letters 'oi' are pronounced 'wa', like in the word *moi*.

---

 1 Write these numbers in figures.

a cinquante-cinq   _____55_____

b soixante-deux   _____

c vingt et un   _____

d trente-neuf   _____

e vingt-quatre   _____

f quarante-sept   _____

g cinquante-huit   _____

h trente-trois   _____

i soixante et un   _____

j quarante-six   _____

Draw lines to link the times to the clocks.

a cinq heures et quart

b trois heures vingt-cinq

c dix heures dix

d six heures et demie

e huit heures moins dix

f cinq heures moins le quart

g neuf heures moins le quart

h onze heures vingt

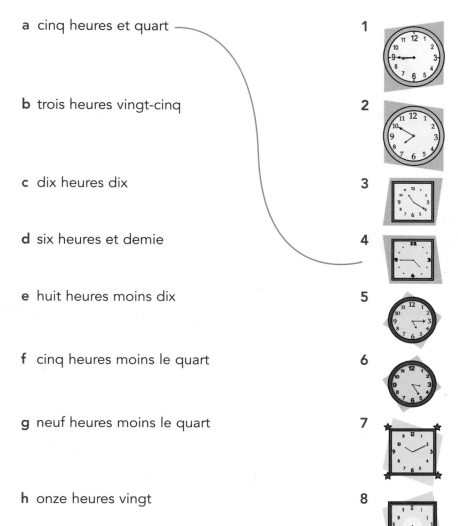

Match up these times which are written using the 12- and 24-hour clock.

1 une heure
2 quatre heures
3 huit heures
4 trois heures
5 deux heures
6 six heures

a quinze heures
b dix-huit heures
c quatorze heures
d treize heures
e seize heures
f vingt heures

Work in pairs. Write down six times. A asks the question: *Quelle heure est-il?* B says the time and A writes it down. When you have finished, check that B has understood the times correctly. Then swap roles.

5 Write down whether it's morning, afternoon, evening or night. Write *C'est le matin / l'après-midi / le soir / la nuit.*

a    _C'est la nuit._

b    _____

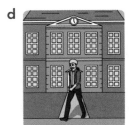

c    _____

d   _____

6 Add hands to these clock faces to show the time.

a Il est trois heures et demie.

b Il est onze heures moins le quart.

c Il est vingt heures vingt.

d Il est vingt et une heures quarante-cinq.

e Il est une heure et quart.

f Il est six heures moins dix.

a   b    c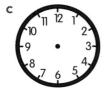

d   e    f

7 Write down the times in these countries.

Au Vietnam, il est vingt heures. En Angleterre, il est treize heures. En France, il est quatorze heures. Au Canada, il est huit heures. Au Sénégal, il est treize heures.

Vietnam: __20:00__   England: _____   France: _____

Canada: _____   Senegal: _____

8 Write out these times in French. ⭐

a 10:40   _Il est onze heures moins vingt._

b 8:15   _____

c 2:45   _____

d 7:30   _____

e 4:25   _____

f 3:35   _____

• Pupil Book pages 38–39

Aujourd'hui, c'est le _____ . Il est _____ .

Langue et grammaire

Using reflexive verbs

A reflexive verb is just the same as any other verb, but also has a small word called a reflexive pronoun which comes before it. These sorts of verbs are often actions that you do to yourself.

je **me** lève	I get up
tu **te** lèves	you get up
il **se** lève	he gets up
elle **se** lève	she gets up
on **se** lève	we get up

The reflexive pronoun is shortened when it comes before a vowel or before the silent *h*:

je **m'**habille	I get dressed

Saying what time you do something

Use the preposition *à* to say what time you do something:

Tu te lèves à quelle heure? What time do you get up?
Je me lève à huit heures. I get up at eight o'clock.

Negatives

To say that you never do something, use *ne ... jamais* around the verb. Note that the reflexive pronoun is included inside the *ne ... jamais*:

*Je **ne** joue **jamais** dans le jardin.* I never play in the garden.

*Je **ne** me lève **jamais** à six heures.* I never get up at six o'clock.

 1 Find all seven words for the days of the week in this grid. Write them out in French.

1 _____
2 _____
3 _____
4 _____
5 _____
6 _____
7 _____

m	a	t	o	h	l	n	s	m
e	l	j	e	u	u	p	l	e
r	m	p	f	g	n	e	r	r
c	a	j	e	u	d	i	s	m
r	r	s	u	r	i	t	a	w
e	j	d	l	m	d	q	m	k
d	i	m	a	n	c	h	e	v
i	v	e	n	d	r	e	d	i
l	b	i	m	a	r	d	i	y

2 Draw lines to link the pictures to the expressions.

Je quitte la maison.

Je me couche.

Je m'habille.

Je rentre chez moi.

Je mange le petit déjeuner.

Je me lève.

3 In the boxes by the pictures in exercise 2, write in the logical time.

| 7h | 7h30 | 8h | 8h30 | 16h | 22h30 |

4 Unjumble these questions and write them down.

a quelle te à Tu heure? lèves

Tu te lèves à quelle heure?

b tu déjeuner? petit À heure le quelle manges

_____

c tu heure t'habilles? quelle À

_____

d heure quittes À maison? la tu quelle

_____

e à chez heure? quelle rentres Tu toi

_____

f quelle te À couches? tu heure

_____

5 Ask a partner the questions you unjumbled in exercise 4 and note down the times. Then swap roles.

6 Use *ne … jamais* to say you never do these things:

a Je renverse mon chocolat chaud.

Je ne renverse jamais mon chocolat chaud.

b Je rate le train.

_____

c J'oublie mes devoirs.

_____

d Je tombe dans ma chambre.

_____

e Je casse mon portable.

_____

7 Write down, in English, six things that prove how lazy this person is.

Zzzz...

> Je ne me lève jamais à sept heures. Je me lève à onze heures.
> Je ne quitte jamais la maison. Je mange le petit déjeuner à midi.
> Je ne m'habille jamais. Je me couche à dix-huit heures.

She never gets up at _____

_____

_____

_____

_____

_____

8 Adapt the sentences in exercise 2 and write an account of a typical day for you. At what time do you do what?

_____

_____

_____

_____

_____

_____

• Pupil Book pages 40–41

Aujourd'hui, c'est le _____ . Il est 🕙 _____ .

Langue et grammaire

Talking about school subjects

To talk about what subjects you have on a particular school day, use the verb *avoir* together with the word for the subject **without** *le/la/les*:

Lundi, j'ai français.	On Monday, I have French.
Mardi, il a maths.	On Tuesday, he has maths.
Vendredi, elle a sciences.	On Friday, she has science.
Jeudi, on a géographie.	On Thursday, we have geography.

To talk about which school subjects you like or don't like, use the word for the school subject **with** the definite article (*le/la/les*):

J'aime le français.	I like French.

Days of the week

Days of the week are written without a capital letter unless they begin a sentence.

Lundi, j'ai maths et	On Monday, I have maths and
mardi, j'ai français.	on Tuesday, I have French.

Pronunciation

Notice how the letters of the alphabet are pronounced differently in French. For example, *EPS* is pronounced 'euh pay ess'.

 1 Write the French subjects in the grid. What is the mystery subject in the tinted boxes? Translate it into English.

1   2

3   4

5   6

7   8

1 | m | a | t | h | s |
2
3
4
5
6
7
8

Mystery subject: _____ = _____

2 Draw lines to link the French and English expressions.

J'aime   I don't like

Je n'aime pas   easy

J'adore   boring

Je déteste   difficult

J'aime beaucoup   I hate

facile   I like a lot

difficile   I like

ennuyeux   I love

3 Write in names.

Léa — J'aime l'informatique, c'est cool. J'adore l'anglais mais je n'aime pas les maths.

Saïd — Je déteste la géographie parce que c'est difficile. J'aime beaucoup la musique et j'adore l'histoire.

Margot — J'adore le français parce que c'est facile. Je n'aime pas beaucoup l'EPS et je déteste les sciences. C'est ennuyeux.

a Who doesn't like maths? _____ Léa _____

b Who really likes music? _____

c Who hates learning about other countries? _____

d Who loves finding out about the past? _____

e Who is a fan of computers? _____

f Who isn't sporty? _____

g Who loves English? _____

h Who isn't at all scientific? _____

4 Tell your partner your opinion of three school subjects. Use *j'aime / je n'aime pas / j'adore / je déteste*. Give reasons, using *parce que c'est facile / difficile / ennuyeux / nul*. Then say *Et toi?* and see what your partner has to say.

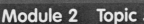

5 Look at the timetable. Put a tick by the true sentences and a cross by the false ones.

a Le jeudi, on a maths. ✓

b Le lundi, on a français.

c Le jeudi, on a histoire.

d Le vendredi, on a informatique.

e Le mardi, on a théâtre.

f Le lundi, on a sciences.

g Le jeudi, et le vendredi on a géographie.

h Le mercredi, on a technologie.

	lundi	mardi	mercredi	jeudi	vendredi
8h	histoire	anglais	musique	arts plastiques	maths
9h	géographie	français	sciences	maths	sciences
10h	technologie	théâtre	français	histoire	informatique
11h	EPS	EPS	anglais	géographie	informatique

6 Write five true sentences about the timetable in exercise 5. Don't use any of the sentences in the exercise!

Le lundi, on a _____

_____

_____

_____

7 In pairs, ask and answer questions about the timetable in exercise 5. ⭐

Exemple
A Qu'est-ce qu'on a le mardi à dix heures?
B Le mardi à dix heures, on a théâtre.

8 Write sentences about the subjects you have on each day in real life. ⭐

Exemple
Le lundi, à neuf heures, on a… À dix heures, on a _____

_____

_____

• Pupil Book pages 42–43

Aujourd'hui, c'est le _____ . Il est _____ .

Langue et grammaire

Talking about what someone else does

To talk about what another person does, use the third person singular of a verb (the form we use for 'he' or 'she'). It is the same form that you have been using with *on*. Look at these examples:

Il quitte la maison.	He leaves the house.
Elle regarde la télé.	She watches TV.
Il fait ses devoirs.	He does homework.

Remember that reflexive verbs have a reflexive pronoun before the verb:

Je me lève.	I get up.
Il se couche.	He goes to bed.
Elle s'habille.	She gets dressed.

 Write in *me*, *se* or *te* (or *m'*, *s'* or *t'*).

a Je ___me___ couche.

b Elle _____ lève.

c Tu _____ habilles.

d Je _____ habille.

e Il _____ couche.

f On _____ lève.

g On _____ habille.

h Elle _____ habille.

i Martine _____ couche.

j Tu _____ lèves.

2 Write in the times.

a Quand il est onze heures à Paris, il est dix-sept heures à Hanoï.

PARIS: __11h__

HANOÏ: _____h

b Quand il est sept heures à Lyon, il est quinze heures en Nouvelle-Calédonie.

LYON: _____h

NOUVELLE-CALÉDONIE: _____h

c Quand il est neuf heures au Canada, il est quatorze heures au Sénégal.

CANADA: _____h

SÉNÉGAL: _____h

3 Now write two sentences like those in exercise 2.

a ANGLETERRE: FRANCE:

b VIETNAM:    MARTINIQUE:

4 Unjumble these sentences.

a se à 11 heures dix couche.

_Il se_ _____

b On sept lève heures se à

_____

c et français J'ai heures à onze demie

_____

d devoirs ses Adrian à fait heures dix-huit

_____

e regardes Tu télé heures vingt la à

_____

5 Read the text and fill in the subjects in the timetable. Write them in English.

Marc a géographie à onze heures.
Quand Marc a géographie, Sandrine a anglais.

Sandrine a informatique à neuf heures.
Quand Sandrine a informatique, Marc a technologie.

Marc a histoire à douze heures.
Quand Marc a histoire, Sandrine a EPS.

Sandrine a sciences à dix heures.
Quand Sandrine a sciences, Marc a musique.

	Sandrine	Marc
9h		
10h		
11h	English	
12h		

6 With a partner, take it in turns to point at a picture and ask *Qu'est-ce qu'il/elle fait?*

Exemple

A Qu'est-ce qu'il fait?

B Il regarde la télé.

| Il/Elle | se lève/se couche/quitte la maison/fait ses devoirs/regarde la télé. |

7 Use the table to help you to translate the sentences below into French. ⭐

Adam	quitte la maison	à six heures.
Manon	se lève	à sept heures.
Camille	fait ses devoirs	à vingt heures.
Nathan	s'habille	à vingt-trois heures.
Raphaël	se couche	à cinq heures.
Yasmine	regarde la télé	à huit heures.

a Yasmine gets up at 6 o'clock.

Yasmine se lève

b Raphaël does homework at 5 o'clock.

c Nathan watches TV at 8 p.m.

d Camille gets dressed at 7 o'clock.

e Adam goes to bed at 11 p.m.

f Manon leaves the house at 8 o'clock.

● Pupil Book pages 56–57

Aujourd'hui, c'est le _____ . Il est _____ .

Langue et grammaire

Plural verbs

To talk about what more than one person does, use the plural form of a verb:

nous parlons	we speak/talk
vous parlez	you speak/talk
ils/elles parlent	they speak/talk

'They' can be *ils* or *elles*.

- Use *ils* to talk about
  - a group of people that includes at least one male
  - masculine plural nouns (or a group of masculine and feminine nouns)
- Use *elles* to talk about
  - a group of women
  - feminine plural nouns

More irregular verbs

You've met the irregular verbs *avoir* and *être*. In this topic, you'll be using the two irregular verbs below. Can you spot the irregularity?

faire	to do
je fais	nous faisons
tu fais	vous faites
il/elle/on fait	ils/elles font

nettoyer	to clean
je nettoie	nous nettoyons
tu nettoies	vous nettoyez
il/elle/on nettoie	ils/elles nettoient

Pronunciation

When you say *ils parlent* or *elles parlent*, you do not pronounce the *–ent* at the end. This means that *parle*, *parles* and *parlent* all sound the same.

---

1   Match the pictures to the activities.

a   J'arrose les plantes.

b   Je fais la vaisselle.

c   Je fais les courses.

d   Je nettoie l'aquarium.

e   Je range ma chambre.

f   Je fais mes devoirs.

2 Complete the sentences by choosing the French equivalent of the word in brackets.

> ne … jamais   toujours   souvent   quelquefois   normalement

a <u>Normalement</u>, je fais la vaisselle. (normally)

b J'arrose _____ les plantes. (often)

c Je fais _____ mes devoirs. (always)

d Je range _____ ma chambre. (sometimes)

e Je fais _____ les courses. (often)

f Je _____ nettoie _____ l'aquarium. (never)

3 Choose the correct form of each verb by crossing out the incorrect option.

a Ils regardent/~~regardons~~ le film.

b Nous dînent/dînons à 7h.

c Il loue/loues un film.

d Elles se dispute/disputent toujours.

e Je parlent/parle avec ma sœur.

f Nous font/faisons nos devoirs.

g Ils arrosons/arrosent les plantes.

h Elles faisons/font les courses.

4 Complete the sentences with the correct form of the verb in brackets.

a Je _____ anglais. (parler)

b Mes parents _____ un film. (louer)

c Nous _____ la télé dans le salon. (regarder)

d Mon frère _____ la vaisselle. (faire)

e Nous _____ une pizza. (commander)

f Mon frère et ma sœur se _____. (disputer)

5 Read these words out loud, concentrating on the endings.

a parle, parlons, parlent, parles

b regardent, regarde, regardez, regardes

c nettoies, nettoyons, nettoient, nettoyez

d fais, faites, faisons, font

e dîne, dînez, dînes, dînent

6 In pairs. A asks *Qu'est-ce que tu fais normalement le week-end?* B replies, giving three activities. If you need extra vocabulary, use a dictionary or ask your teacher. Then swap roles.

7 Read Emma's speech bubble. Then, for each activity, write 'I', 'we', 'she' or 'they'. ⭐

a _I_ like Friday.

b ___ do homework.

c ___ tidy bedroom.

d ___ argue.

e ___ go for a walk.

f ___ watch a film.

g ___ water the plants.

h ___ order a pizza.

Moi, le week-end, j'aime le vendredi soir. Normalement, nous commandons une pizza et nous regardons un film à la télé. Souvent, nos parents se disputent – hélas. Le samedi, je fais mes devoirs et ma sœur range sa chambre. C'est difficile, ça. Le dimanche, j'arrose quelquefois les plantes et nous nous promenons dans le parc.

8 Translate the sentences into French. ⭐

a We do the washing up. _____

b They watch a film. _____

c I tidy my bedroom. _____

d We go shopping. _____

e They order a pizza. _____

f I do my homework. _____

• Pupil Book pages 58–59

Aujourd'hui, c'est le [calendar] _____ . Il est [clock] _____ .

Langue et grammaire

The verb *aller* (to go)

Aller is another irregular verb. Look at how it is formed:

je vais	I go / am going
tu vas	you go / are going
il va	he goes / is going
elle va	she goes / is going
nous allons	we go / are going
vous allez	you go / are going
ils/elles vont	they go / are going

How to say 'to the'

Use *à la* when the place you are going to is feminine.
Use *au* when the place you are going to is masculine.
Use *aux* when the place you are going to is plural.
Use *à l'* when the place begins with a vowel or silent 'h'.

Elle va à la plage.	She's going to the beach.
Je vais au parc.	I'm going to the park.
Il va aux magasins.	He's going to the shops.
Nous allons à l'église.	We're going to the church.

1 For each location, write *au*, *à la* or *aux*.

a _____à la_____ plage

b _____ piscine

c _____ magasins

d _____ centre d'équitation

e _____ cinéma

f _____ parc

g _____ skate-parc

h _____ collège

2 Circle the correct forms of *aller*.

a nous allez / (allons)

b il vais / va

c vous allez / allons

d je vas / vais

e tu vas / vais

f elle va / vas

g ils vont / allons

h elles va / vont

3 For each sentence, write the correct form of *aller*.

a Je ___vais___ au skate-parc.

b Nous _____ au collège.

c Elle _____ à la piscine.

d Elles _____ au centre d'équitation.

e Papa _____ aux magasins.

f Maman _____ au parc.

4 Complete the conversations using *au*, *à la* or *à l'*.

a Tu vas *au parc*?

   Non, je vais _____.

b Tu vas _____ _____ ?

   Non, je vais _____ _____.

c Tu vas _____ _____ ?

   Non, je vais _____ _____.

5 In pairs. B thinks of a place to go and writes it down. A asks questions to find out what it is. When A has guessed correctly, swap roles.

A Tu vas _____ _____?

B Non.

A Tu vas _____ _____?

6 Unjumble these sentences.

a préfère la Je à piscine aller _____

b magasins préfère aux aller Je _____

c aller au Je cinéma préfère _____

d la plage à Je aller préfère _____

e aller Je aux préfère magasins _____

f parc préfère aller Je au _____

7 Read Simon's email then fill in the gaps in the sentences below. ⭐

Salut Rachid,

Qu'est-ce que tu préfères faire le week-end? Moi, je vais souvent aux magasins parce que je pense que c'est intéressant. Mais je préfère aller à la plage parce que je trouve que c'est tranquille et amusant. Et toi?

Amitiés,
Simon

Simon often goes _____ because it's _____. But he prefers _____ because he thinks it's _____ and _____.

8 Reply to Simon's email. Mention at least two things you often do or like doing and say why. If you need more vocabulary, use a dictionary or ask your teacher. ⭐

● Pupil Book pages 60–61

Aujourd'hui, c'est le _____ . Il est _____ .

Langue et grammaire

Talking about sport

Use *faire* (to do) or *jouer* (to play) to talk about doing different sports.

For sports that are masculine use *faire du* or *jouer au*:
Je fais du roller.
Je joue au basket.

For sports that are feminine use *faire de la* or *jouer à la*:

Je fais de la danse.
Je joue à la pétanque.

Remember, if the sport begins with a vowel use *l'*:
Je fais de l'escrime.

Talking about what you can do

Use *on peut* with *faire* or *jouer* to talk about what you **can** do.

Au centre sportif on peut jouer au tennis. — At the sports centre you can play tennis.
On peut faire de la boxe. — You can do boxing.

 1 Solve the picture clues and find the French words in the grid.

E	P	T	M	C	P	D	S	F	K
Q	N	É	B	S	K	A	T	E	M
B	A	I	T	M	O	G	E	S	X
F	O	J	P	A	E	S	L	C	Z
U	T	X	O	I	N	È	W	R	B
T	N	G	E	A	Y	Q	D	I	A
S	É	M	D	L	P	T	U	M	S
A	H	K	A	E	O	V	B	E	K
L	S	T	E	N	N	I	S	D	E
L	H	A	N	D	B	A	L	L	T

a _____

b _____

c  _____

d _____

e _____

f  _____

g _____

h _____

i _____

2 For each sentence, choose *Je joue* or *Je fais*. Think about what you would say in English in each case. Cross out the incorrect words.

a ~~Je joue~~ / Je fais de la boxe.

b Je joue / Je fais au rugby.

c Je joue / Je fais au tennis.

d Je joue / Je fais de l'escrime.

e Je joue / Je fais au basket.

f Je joue / Je fais à la pétanque.

g Je joue / Je fais du roller.

h Je joue / Je fais au handball.

3 Write in *au*, *à la*, *à l'*, *du*, *de la* or *de l'*.

a Je joue ____au____ rugby.

c Je joue _____ tennis.

e Je joue _____ futsal.

g Je fais _____ escrime.

b Je fais _____ danse.

d Je fais _____ skate.

f Je fais _____ roller.

h Je joue _____ basket.

4 Write in the missing words.

a On peut _____ du roller.

b On peut jouer _____ tennis de table.

c On peut _____ au handball.

d On peut faire _____ l'escrime.

e On _____ faire de la danse.

f On peut jouer _____ rugby.

5 Unjumble these sentences.

a peut la On jouer pétanque à   *On peut jouer à la pétanque.*

b faire peut roller On du   _____

c jouer On futsal au peut   _____

d de faire danse la peut On   _____

e minigolf au jouer peut On   _____

6 Imagine you are advertising this sports centre. Tell your partner a few things you can do there, beginning *On peut...*

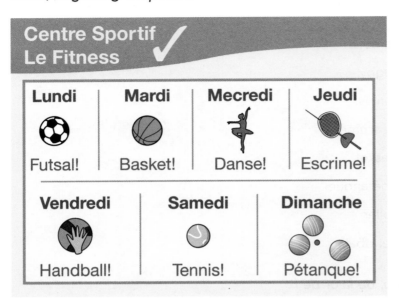

Centre Sportif Le Fitness ✓

Lundi	Mardi	Mecredi	Jeudi
Futsal!	Basket!	Danse!	Escrime!

Vendredi	Samedi	Dimanche
Handball!	Tennis!	Pétanque!

7 Write at least five sentences saying what you can do at the Centre Sportif Le Fitness on which days. ⭐

Le mercredi, on peut faire de la danse.

_____

_____

_____

_____

_____

8 Now translate what you have written in exercise 7 into English. ⭐

_____

_____

_____

_____

_____

• Pupil Book pages 62–63

Aujourd'hui, c'est le _____ . Il est _____ .

Langue et grammaire

Nous allons, nous faisons

Remember that *nous* is always followed by a verb ending in *–ons*:

nous regardons	we watch
nous jouons	we play

The verb *aller* follows the same pattern:

nous allons   we go

Note that the *nous* form of the verb *faire* has an 's':

nous faisons   we do

Talking about the seasons

The word *en* is used to talk about a season, except for spring when you use *au* instead:

en été	in summer
en automne	in autumn
en hiver	in winter
au printemps	in spring

1 Write the French words for these seasons.

a  _____

b  _____

c  _____

d  _____

2 Insert *en* or *au*.

a ____En____ été nous faisons des barbecues.

b _____ hiver nous faisons du ski.

c _____ printemps nous faisons du vélo.

d _____ été nous allons à la plage.

e _____ automne nous faisons des balades à la campagne.

3 Translate these expressions of frequency into English.

French	English
a souvent	often
b quelquefois	
c chaque année	
d une fois par mois	
e deux fois par semaine	
f de temps en temps	

4 Look at the pictures. Describe the activities in French using the words in the box.

a

Nous faisons du vélo.

b

_____

c

_____

d

_____

e

_____

f

_____

| Nous allons | au théâtre | au spectacle | | |
| Nous faisons | un barbecue | une balade | du vélo | du ski |

5 Use the grid to make sentences saying what you do, how often and in which season.

De temps en temps	nous faisons du ski	au printemps
Chaque année	nous allons à une exposition	en été
Deux fois par mois	nous allons au cinéma	en automne
Une fois par semaine	nous faisons une balade	en hiver

Chaque année en hiver nous faisons du ski.

_____

_____

6 Read the sentences you wrote in exercise 5 out loud to a partner.

 7 Read this post on the *Forum des francophones* and complete the sentences in English. ⭐

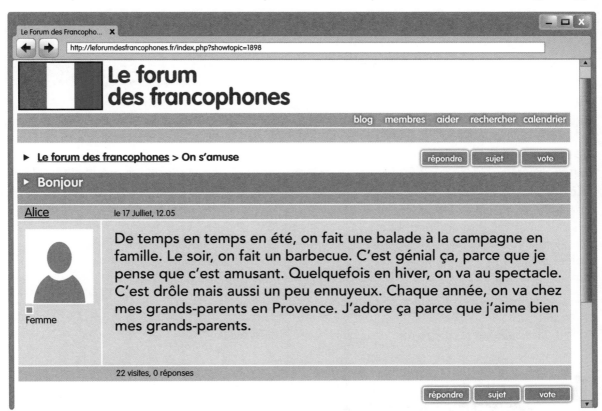

Le Forum des Francopho... ✕

http://leforumdesfrancophones.fr/index.php?showtopic=1898

Le forum des francophones

blog   membres   aider   rechercher   calendrier

▶ **Le forum des francophones** > On s'amuse

répondre   sujet   vote

▶ **Bonjour**

Alice   le 17 Julliet, 12.05

Femme

De temps en temps en été, on fait une balade à la campagne en famille. Le soir, on fait un barbecue. C'est génial ça, parce que je pense que c'est amusant. Quelquefois en hiver, on va au spectacle. C'est drôle mais aussi un peu ennuyeux. Chaque année, on va chez mes grands-parents en Provence. J'adore ça parce que j'aime bien mes grands-parents.

22 visites, 0 réponses

répondre   sujet   vote

a From time to time ___in summer___, we go _____.

b In the evening, we _____.

c I think it's _____ because _____.

d Sometimes _____.

e I think it's _____ but _____.

f Each year, _____.

g I _____ that because _____.

 8 Write a paragraph about

- what you sometimes do in summer
- what you do often
- what you think of those activities. ⭐

• Pupil Book pages 64–65

Aujourd'hui, c'est le _____ . Il est 🕐 _____ .

Langue et grammaire

Talking about what belongs to someone

In English, you use the letter 's' to talk about what belongs to someone. For example, 'Marie's brother'. In French, use *de* (or *d'* before a vowel) like this:

le frère de Marie   la guitare d'Abdou   l'anniversaire de Sophie

Months and dates

Like the days of the week, the months of the year are written without a capital letter in French.

To say that your birthday is in a particular month use *en* before the month:

Mon anniversaire est en mai.   My birthday is in May.

To say that your birthday is on a particular date use *le* before the date:

Mon anniversaire est le quinze mai.   My birthday is on 15 May.

Abbreviations

It is very common in French for long words to be shortened by dropping one or more syllables at the end. The word *anniversaire* is a good example – sometimes it's shortened to just *anniv*.

Boire

The verb *boire* (to drink) is another important irregular verb:

je bois	I drink
tu bois	you drink
il/elle boit	he/she drinks
on boit	we drink

 Insert the French words for the months into the crossword.

Across

1 August
2 February
5 July
7 December
8 May
9 November
11 January

Down

1 April
3 October
4 September
6 June
10 March

2 Write these dates in figures.

a le sept novembre ___7/11___

b le quinze février _____

c le douze avril _____

d le vingt-cinq octobre _____

e le treize août _____

f le quatorze septembre _____

g le vingt et un juillet _____

h le neuf mai _____

3 Ask at least five people in your class *C'est quand ton anniversaire?* Note down the dates in figures. Check you've got them right!

4 Read the text. Write out each person's birthday in English.

> Les anniversaires de mes copains
>
> L'anniversaire de Gabriel est le onze octobre.
> L'anniversaire de Louis est le quinze janvier.
> L'anniversaire de Claire est le vingt-deux août.
> L'anniversaire de Lina est le treize mars.
> L'anniversaire de Roland est le trente avril et
> l'anniversaire de Farah est le douze décembre.

Gabriel ___11th October___

Louis _____

Claire _____

Lina _____

Roland _____

Farah _____

5 Translate these expressions of time into French.

finalement   ensuite   après   d'abord

a first d'_____

b after that _____

c then _____

d finally _____

6 In what order are these activities mentioned? Number them 1–7.

Watching a DVD _____

Dancing _____

Listening to music ___1___

Eating crisps _____

Going home _____

Eating cake _____

Playing on the computer _____

> À la fête d'anniversaire, d'abord on écoute de la musique et on danse. Ensuite, on mange du gâteau et des chips. Après, on regarde un DVD ou on joue sur l'ordinateur. Finalement, on rentre à la maison.

7 Match the beginnings and ends of the sentences to make a description of a birthday outing.

Mon anniversaire,   mes copains au centre sportif.

Souvent, j'invite   on boit du coca.

D'abord,   c'est le dix juin.

Ensuite,   chez nous.

Après, on mange   des hot-dogs et du gâteau d'anniversaire.

Finalement, on rentre   on fait du skate.

8 Write a description of a typical birthday party. ⭐

> D'abord / ensuite / après / finalement
> On danse / écoute de la musique / chante
> On mange des chips / des pizzas / des hot-dogs / du gâteau
> On boit du cola / du jus de fruit
> On rentre à la maison / va au lit

_____

_____

_____

_____

_____

- Pupil Book pages 66–67

Aujourd'hui, c'est le _____ . Il est _____ .

Langue et grammaire

Choosing from a menu

To say what you'd like to eat, use the verb *prendre* (to take). *Prendre* is an irregular verb. Look at how it works:

je prends	I take
tu prends	you take
il/elle prend	he/she takes

Here are some examples:

Qu'est-ce que tu prends? What are you having?
Je prends une pizza. I'm having a pizza.

How to say 'some'

The word for 'some' in French depends upon whether the noun you're talking about is masculine, feminine or plural, or begins with a vowel:

du cola	some cola
du jus de fruit	some fruit juice
de la limonade	some lemonade
de l'eau	some water
des champignons	some mushrooms
des tomates	some tomatoes

1 Write the name of the food or drink item next to each picture.

nouilles   oignon   champignons   œuf   sucre   crêpe   tomate   limonade

a un ___œuf___

b une _____

c des _____

d une _____

e du _____

f de la _____

g des _____

h un _____

2 For each food or drink item, write *du*, *de la*, *de l'* or *des*.

a le sucre ___du sucre___

b l'eau _____

c le jambon _____

d le fromage _____

e les champignons _____

f la limonade _____

3 Read the descriptions and write *sucrée* or *salée*, and whether it's a *crêpe* or a *galette*.

Crêperie Charlie

Sucre 5€   *sucrée, crêpe*

Pommes 6€   _____

Jambon 7€   _____

Tomates et oignons 6€   _____

Jambon et fromage 8€   _____

Chocolat 6€   _____

Champignons 8€   _____

Fromage et œuf 8€   _____

 4 In pairs. A runs Crêperie Charlie. B orders a *galette* and then a *crêpe* for dessert. Then swap roles.

Exemple
A Bonjour.
B Bonjour. Je prends une galette avec du fromage et du jambon et ensuite je prends une crêpe avec des pommes.
A Avec plaisir.

 5 Which restaurant should each person go to? Write numbers 1–4 next to the pictures.

1   Je n'aime pas le fromage mais j'adore les tajines.

a   Pizzeria San Marco

_____

2   J'adore les galettes et j'aime le chocolat.

b   Crêperie Charlie

_____

3   J'aime beaucoup les nouilles.

c   RESTAURANT TAJINE

_____

4   Je déteste les nouilles mais j'aime beaucoup les tomates.

d   RESTAURANT HANOÏ

_____

6 In pairs. A finds out what foods B likes and dislikes by asking *Tu aimes le / la / les...?*
B replies: *Oui, j'aime / j'aime beaucoup / j'adore...* or *Non, je n'aime pas / je déteste...*
Then swap roles.

7 Read Michel's email and answer the questions in English. ⭐

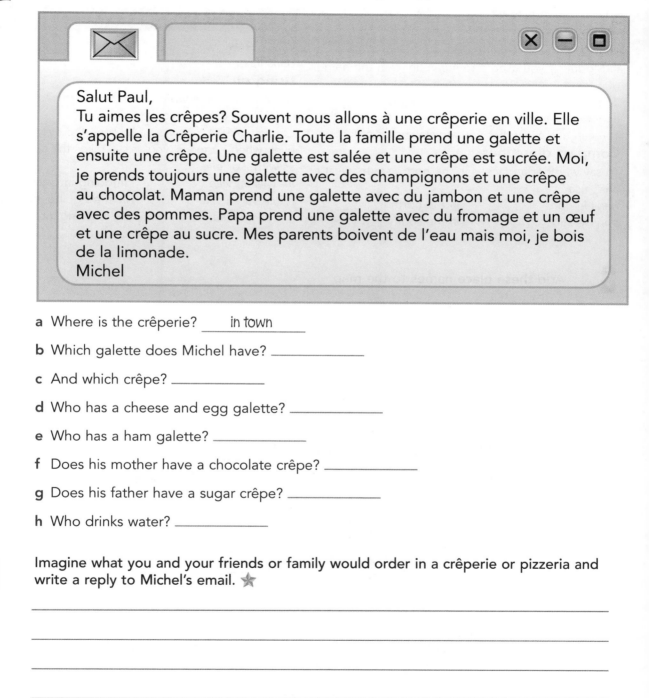

Salut Paul,
Tu aimes les crêpes? Souvent nous allons à une crêperie en ville. Elle s'appelle la Crêperie Charlie. Toute la famille prend une galette et ensuite une crêpe. Une galette est salée et une crêpe est sucrée. Moi, je prends toujours une galette avec des champignons et une crêpe au chocolat. Maman prend une galette avec du jambon et une crêpe avec des pommes. Papa prend une galette avec du fromage et un œuf et une crêpe au sucre. Mes parents boivent de l'eau mais moi, je bois de la limonade.
Michel

a Where is the crêperie? _____in town_____

b Which galette does Michel have? _____

c And which crêpe? _____

d Who has a cheese and egg galette? _____

e Who has a ham galette? _____

f Does his mother have a chocolate crêpe? _____

g Does his father have a sugar crêpe? _____

h Who drinks water? _____

8 Imagine what you and your friends or family would order in a crêperie or pizzeria and write a reply to Michel's email. ⭐

_____

_____

_____

_____

_____

4 Topic 1 Connais-tu la France?

- Pupil Book pages 80–81

Aujourd'hui, c'est le _____ . Il est _____ .

Langue et grammaire

Using à
In Module 1 you used à to mean 'in' with the name of a town. It can also mean 'to':
Je suis à Paris. — I am in Paris.
Je vais à Marseille. — I am going to Marseille.
You can use à whether you are staying or going.

Compass directions
To say whether a place is in the north, south, west or east, use:
dans le nord — in the north
dans le sud — in the south
dans l'ouest — in the west
dans l'est — in the east

Using on
You have met the word *on* before. In this topic, it is used like a general 'you':
On voit la Seine. — You see the river Seine.
Even when it means 'you' it still takes the same form as with *il* or *elle*.
Je vais en ville. — I'm going into town.
Il/elle va en ville. — He/she's going into town.
On va en ville. — You're going into town.

 1 Add these place names to the map.

Paris	Marseille	Nice	Lille	Nantes
les Alpes	les Pyrénées	le Massif Central	la Seine	la Loire

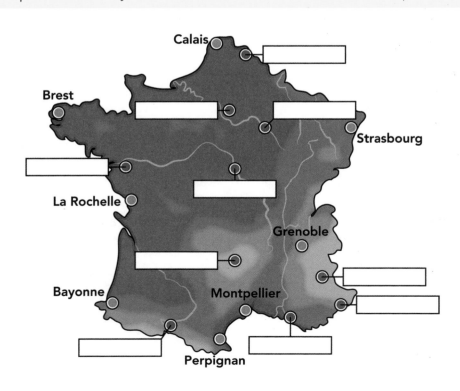

2 Refer to the map and complete these sentences.
Write *nord*, *sud*, *est* or *ouest*.

a Calais est dans le _____nord_____ de la France.

b La Rochelle est dans l' _____ de la France.

c Brest est dans l' _____ de la France.

d Grenoble est dans l' _____ de la France.

e Strasbourg est dans l' _____ de la France.

f Montpellier est dans le _____ de la France.

g Bayonne est dans le _____ de la France.

h Perpignan est dans le _____ de la France.

3 Copy the right phrase next to each picture.

| à la montagne | au bord de la mer | à la campagne | en ville |

a

à la _____

b

_____

c

_____

d

_____

4 Read this blog extract and answer the questions with 'yes' or 'no'.

▶ **Escapades**

le 26 julliet, 12h05

Salut! Je m'appelle Sandrine et j'habite à St-Julien. St-Julien est à la campagne, près de Marseille. Marseille est au bord de la mer, dans le sud de la France. Quand on aime les grandes villes, on va à Marseille.

a Does Sandrine live in a town? _____no_____

b Is St-Julien a big city? _____

c Is Marseille by the sea? _____

d Is Marseille in the north? _____

e Does Sandrine live in Marseille? _____

f Is St-Julien near Marseille? _____

5 Complete the sentences with *vais*, *vas* or *va*.

a Je _____vais_____ en ville.

b Magali _____ à la montagne?

c Oui, elle _____ à Grenoble.

d Tu _____ au bord de la mer?

e Non, je _____ à Paris.

f Jean-Marc _____ en Ardèche.

6 Unjumble the sentences and write them out correctly. ★

a en va ville Elle

_____Elle va_____

b vais Je bord au mer la de

_____

c On Paris à est

_____

d est Il la à campagne

_____

7 Now translate the sentences in exercise 6 into English. ★

a _She's going_____

b _____

c _____

d _____

• Pupil Book pages 82–83

Aujourd'hui, c'est le _____ . Il est _____ .

Langue et grammaire

Asking questions

One useful word when asking questions in French is *quel(le)*. Use *quel* with a masculine word and *quelle* with a feminine word:

C'est quel genre de parc?	What kind of park is it?
C'est quelle saison?	Which season is it?

Although the masculine and the feminine forms are spelled differently, they are pronounced the same. *Quand?* and *où?* are also very useful words when asking questions in French.

Tu vas où?	Where are you going?
Tu vas quand?	When are you going?

Using *aller* to talk about the future

A simple way of expressing the future in French is to use *aller* in the present tense followed by the infinitive of the verb you want to use:

Je vais aller à Disneyland.	I'm going to go to Disneyland
Ça va être sympa!	It's going to be nice!

Pronunciation

Remember, when a verb ends in *–ent*, the ending is not pronounced. For example, *ils aiment*.

 1 Draw lines to link the pictures with the sentences.

a C'est pour les personnes qui aiment les montagnes russes.

1

b C'est pour les personnes qui aiment l'histoire.

2

c C'est pour les personnes qui aiment les volcans.

3

d C'est pour les personnes qui aiment l'espace.

4

e C'est pour les personnes qui aiment la mer.

5

2 When are these months? Write *en hiver, en été, en automne* or *au printemps.*

a août   _____en été_____

b octobre   _____

c septembre   _____

d janvier   _____

e décembre   _____

f juillet   _____

g mars   _____

h avril   _____

3 Which French parks would have these equivalents? Write in the French park name.

a Volcano Land!   _____

b Space City!   _____

c Sea World!   _____

4 Ask several people these questions. Answer the questions they ask you. Write down your answers.

C'est quand, ton anniversaire?   _____

C'est en quelle saison?   _____

5 Unjumble these words to make questions.

a vas aller Tu où?   _____Tu vas aller où?_____

b parc? C'est genre quel de   _____

c saison? en C'est quelle   _____

d vas Tu aller y quand?   _____

e dans C'est région quelle?   _____

6 Read this conversation and answer the English questions.

Emma Tu vas aller où?

Hugo Je vais aller au Futuroscope.

Emma C'est dans quelle région?

Hugo C'est près de Poitiers.

Emma C'est quel genre de parc?

Hugo C'est pour les personnes qui aiment les sciences.

Emma Tu vas y aller quand?

Hugo En été … en juillet.

a What is Futuroscope?   It's _____

b Where is it?   _____

c Who will like it?   _____

d When is Hugo going?   _____

7 Find the French questions in exercise 6 and write them down. ⭐

a What sort of park is it?   C'est quel _____

b What region is it in?   _____

c Where are you going to go?   _____

d When are you going to go there?   _____

8 Have a conversation like the one in exercise 6 with a partner. Try to vary your answers. You could research French theme parks on the internet. ⭐

_____

_____

_____

• Pupil Book pages 84–85

Aujourd'hui, c'est le ⬜ _____ . Il est 🕐 _____ .

Langue et grammaire

Talking about being hungry, thirsty or scared

To say you are hungry, thirsty or scared, use the verb *avoir*:

J'ai faim.	I'm hungry.
J'ai soif.	I'm thirsty.
J'ai peur.	I'm scared.

To say you are not hungry, thirsty or scared, use the phrase *je n'ai pas*. Remember that *ne* always comes before the verb and *pas* always comes after:

Je **n'ai** **pas** *faim.*   I'm not hungry.

To ask friends if they are hungry, thirsty or scared, use *Tu as...?*

Tu as soif?	Are you hungry?

Or you could use *Tu n'as pas...?*:

Tu n'as pas peur?	Aren't you scared?

Remember that when you ask a question in French your voice must go up at the end. Listen carefully to the audio and copy the intonation when you ask questions.

Intensifiers

If you want to provide a more precise answer, you can add phrases such as *pas du tout* (not at all), *un peu* (a little), *très* (very) or *trop* (too or too much):

J'ai très soif.	I am very thirsty.
Je n'ai pas du tout faim.	I am not hungry at all.

---

1 Complete the explanation in English for each speech bubble.

1 J'ai faim.　　　　This person is ____hungry____ .

2 Je n'ai pas soif.　　　　This person is _____ .

3 J'ai peur.　　　　This person is _____ .

4 J'ai soif.　　　　This person is _____ .

5 Je n'ai pas peur.　　　　This person is _____ .

6 Je n'ai pas faim.　　　　This person is _____ .

2 Write in the appropriate French word.

a J'ai _____peur_____ .

b J'ai _____ .

c Je n'ai pas _____ .

d Je n'ai pas _____ .

e J'ai _____ .

3 Monsieur and Madame Contraire never agree on anything. Fill in the gaps.

a M. Contraire   J'ai faim.

Mme Contraire   Je n'ai _____ .

b M. Contraire   J'ai soif.

Mme Contraire   Je _____ .

c M. Contraire   J'ai peur.

Mme Contraire   Je _____ .

4 Draw lines to match questions 1–3 with answers a–c.

1 Tu as soif?

2 Tu as faim?

3 Tu as peur?

a Oui, je voudrais un sandwich.

b Oui! Au secours!

c Non, je n'ai pas soif.

5 Number these expressions in **ascending** order, starting with *pas du tout*.

trop _____   très _____   pas du tout _1_   assez _____   un peu _____

6 Ask a few people some questions. Note their answers.

Find out:

- how they are
- whether they are hungry
- whether they are thirsty
- whether they are scared

_____

_____

_____

_____

7 Are these people hungry, thirsty or scared? Write your answer in French. ⭐

a

Je voudrais
une baguette.

Elle a _____.

b Je voudrais
un cola.

_____.

c Je n'aime pas les monstres.
Je voudrais rentrer à la maison!

_____.

8 Write sentences beginning with *Je voudrais...* ⭐

a You're hungry.   Je voudrais _____.

b You're thirsty.   _____.

c Finally, something to say if you're scared.   _____.

- Pupil Book pages 86–87

Aujourd'hui, c'est le _____ . Il est _____ .

Langue et grammaire

Plural verbs

In formal French, use *nous* to mean 'we'. Verbs that come after *nous* end in –*ons*.

nous proposons	we offer / we are offering

In less formal contexts, use *on* to mean 'we':

on joue	we play / we are playing

Use *ils* (or *elles* for groups which are all female) to mean 'they'. The verb usually ends in –*ent*.

ils/elles jouent	they play / they are playing
ils/elles visitent	they visit / they are visiting

Some irregular verbs end in –*ont*:

ils/elles ont	they have
ils/elles vont	they go / they are going
ils/elles font	they do / they are doing

Using the imperative

To give instructions or advice, you need to use the imperative. Use two different forms:

Informal (people you say *tu* to)

Écoute!	Listen!
Regarde!	Look!
Fais attention!	Be careful!

Formal (people you say *vous* to, or more than one person)

Écoutez!	Listen!
Regardez!	Look!
Faites attention!	Be careful!

---

 1   Draw lines to link the words for the pictured activities.

a   avoir —————— des cours   P

b   faire   la voile

c   faire   de la natation

d   faire   aux cartes

e   faire   des balades

f   jouer   de l'équitation

 2   Look again at exercise 1. Write *S* next to singular French nouns and *P* next to plural ones.

3 Decide whether these instructions are being given to one person or two people. Write *1* or *2*.

a Arrête! _____1_____   b Allez en ville. _____

c Écoute la musique. _____   d Va à la maison. _____

e Regardez la télé. _____   f Fais attention! _____

g Attrape le ballon. _____   h Arrêtez! _____

4 Write in the *nous* and the *ils/elles* forms of these verbs.

a j'ai   nous __avons__   ils ___ont___

b Je visite   nous _____   elles _____

c Je fais   nous _____   ils _____

d Je joue   nous _____   elles _____

e Je vais   nous _____   elles _____

5 Work with a partner. A thinks of an activity and writes it down. B guesses what A is planning for the two of you. Continue until B gets it right. Then swap roles.

Exemple

B Nous faisons de la voile?

A Non.

6 Translate these short phrases into French. ⭐

a they (m) are going   __ils vont__

b they (f) are doing   _____

c we visit   _____

d we watch   _____

e they (f) have   _____

f we play   _____

7 Read the text and answer the questions with 'yes' or 'no'.

Séjour linguistique à Paris

Pour les 13–16 ans

Le matin, à partir de 9 heures, ils ont des cours de français avec un professeur bien qualifié. À midi, ils mangent à la cantine. L'après-midi, ils visitent les monuments de Paris. Ils visitent le Louvre et la tour Eiffel. Le soir, ils écoutent de la musique ou regardent un film. C'est un séjour très intéressant.

a Do lessons start at 8 o'clock?   no

b Can 12-year-olds take part?   _____

c Is it happening in London?   _____

d Do they watch films in the afternoon?   _____

e Do they visit the Eiffel Tower?   _____

f Do they have evening activities?   _____

g Is lunch provided?   _____

h Is it suitable for music lovers?   _____

8 Translate these sentences into English. ⭐

a Nous faisons de la planche à voile   *We go windsurfing.*

b Le soir, ils vont au cinéma.   _____

c Le matin, elles font des balades à la campagne.   _____

d L'après-midi, nous avons des cours.   _____

e Elles visitent les monuments.   _____

f Nous faisons de l'équitation.   _____

• Pupil Book pages 88–89

Aujourd'hui, c'est le _____. Il est _____.

Langue et grammaire

Talking about the weather

To ask what the weather is like, use:
Il fait quel temps?
You rarely need the word *temps* in the answer.
Instead say:

Il fait chaud.	It's hot.
Il fait froid.	It's cold.
Il fait beau.	The weather is nice.
Il fait mauvais.	The weather is bad.
Il y a du soleil.	It's sunny.
Il pleut.	It's raining.
Il neige.	It's snowing.

Talking about countries

To introduce the name of a country or a continent, use:
• *en* with feminine names of countries or continents
Le Sénégal est en Afrique. Senegal is in Africa.
Ben va aller en France. Ben is going to go to France.
• *au* with masculine names of countries
Montréal est au Canada. Montreal is in Canada.
Abdou va aller au Sénégal. Abdou is going to go to Senegal.
Unlike in English, you use the same preposition to say both where you are and where you are going to.

 1 Unjumble the French words for these English expressions.

a It's rubbish   eC'ts lun   *C'est nul.*

b not really   sap mavrinte   _____

c not too bad   asp prot lam   _____

d great   éiglan   _____

e as usual   momce hibd'atedu   _____

 2 Circle the correct answer.

a Il pleut   (It's raining.) / It's sunny.

b Il fait beau   It's horrible. / It's nice.

c Il fait froid   It's cold. / It's warm.

d Il fait chaud   It's cold. / It's hot.

e Il neige   It's snowing. / It's raining.

f Il y a du soleil   It's sunny. / It's stormy.

3 Look at the map and complete the French sentences.

a Dans l'ouest de la France, il y a du _____.

b Dans l'est de la France, il _____.

c Dans le sud de la France, il _____.

d Dans le nord de la France, il _____.

4 Write in *en* or *au*.

a Vancouver est ___au___ Canada.

b J'habite _____ Angleterre.

c Rouen est _____ France.

d San Francisco est _____ Amérique.

e Je vais aller _____ Sénégal.

f Annabel habite _____ Tunisie.

5 Unjumble these weather expressions and write them out.

a y Il soleil a du   Il y a du soleil.

b froid Il fait   _____

c chaud fait Il   _____

d Il beau fait   _____

e a y vent Il du   _____

f temps? fait Il quel   _____

6 Read the text. Are the sentences true (T) or false (F)? ⭐

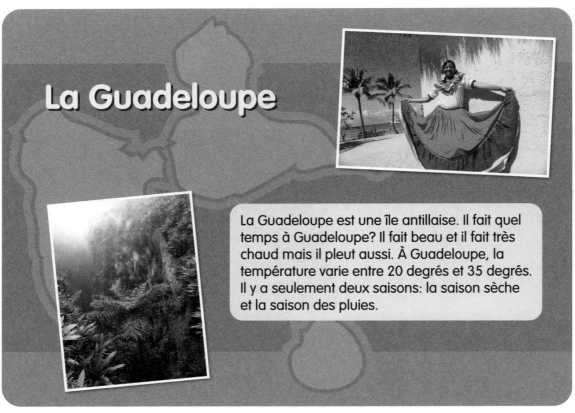

La Guadeloupe

La Guadeloupe est une île antillaise. Il fait quel temps à Guadeloupe? Il fait beau et il fait très chaud mais il pleut aussi. À Guadeloupe, la température varie entre 20 degrés et 35 degrés. Il y a seulement deux saisons: la saison sèche et la saison des pluies.

* antillais(e) = Caribbean

a There are four seasons in Guadeloupe. ___F___

b The weather is often cold. _____

c The temperature can go as high as 40 degrees. _____

d It rains sometimes. _____

e There are only two seasons. _____

f It never goes below 20 degrees. _____

g There's a big problem with snow. _____

h It's a warm climate. _____

7 Make up two weather reports for your own area and write them down in French. ⭐

En été, il _____ .

En hiver, il _____ .

• Pupil Book pages 90–91

Aujourd'hui, c'est le _____ . Il est _____ .

Langue et grammaire

Using *aller*

You have already learned to use the present tense of *aller* followed by a verb in the infinitive to say what you are going to do:

Je vais jouer au foot.   I'm going to play football.

You can use other forms of the verb *aller* to describe what other people plan to do:

je vais	I'm going
tu vas	you're going
il/elle va	he/she/it is going
on va	we're going (informal)
nous allons	we're going
vous allez	you're going
ils/elles vont	they're going
Qu'est-ce que tu vas faire?	What are you going to do?

Je voudrais

To say what you'd like to do, use *je voudrais* followed by a verb in the infinitive:

Je voudrais aller au Maroc.   I'd like to go to Morocco.

Remember that you can also use *je voudrais* followed by a noun:

Je voudrais un sandwich.   I'd like a sandwich.

Pronunciation

Remember that 'th' always sounds like the letter 't' in French, so be careful when you say *un thé à la menthe*.

---

1 Circle the correct translation.

a génial — (brilliant) / terrible / boring

b une semaine — a week / a month / a year

c pourquoi? — where? / when? / why?

d une tajine — taxi / Moroccan dish / target

e nul — rubbish / cool / nut

f partir en vacances — go partying / be vacant / go on holiday

2 Translate these expressions into English.

a une semaine   _____a week_____

b sur la plage   _____

c faire des balades _____

d la planche à voile _____

e dans la mer   _____

f du thé   _____

g sans mes parents _____

h jouer au ballon _____

3   Unjumble these sentences in which someone says what they are going to do.

a vais mer Je semaine passer de bord au une la

Je vais passer une semaine au bord de la mer.

b à vais planche la Je de voile faire

_____

c au la sur jouer vais Je ballon plage

_____

d vais la Je dans nager mer

_____

4   Now re-write the sentences in exercise 3 beginning with _Tu vas ..._

Tu vas _____

_____

_____

_____

5   Now re-write the sentences in exercise 3 beginning with _Je voudrais ..._

Je voudrais passer _____

_____

_____

_____

6 Will these people do these things or **would they like** to do them?
Write 'will' or 'would like'.

a Je voudrais manger un hamburger.   *would like*

b Je vais aller dans le désert.

c Je voudrais faire une balade en ville.

d Tu vas jouer au badminton.

e Tu vas nager dans la mer.

f Je voudrais faire de la planche à voile.

7 Work in pairs. A asks questions starting *Tu vas...?* B replies *Oui, je vais...* or
Non, je ne vais pas... Then swap roles.

Start with these activities:

• jouer au ping-pong?

• aller à Paris?

• manger un gâteau?

8 Write down three things you would like to do, beginning *Je voudrais...* ⭐
You could extend your sentences further by using *pourquoi* to say why.
If you need to use words you haven't learned yet, ask your teacher
or use a dictionary.

• Pupil Book pages 104–105

Aujourd'hui, c'est le _____ . Il est _____ .

Langue et grammaire

Jouer

Remember that *jouer* is the French verb 'to play' and that *jouer à* is used to talk about playing a sport or game. To talk about playing a musical instrument, use *jouer de*. Remember to change the *de* depending on whether the musical instrument is masculine or feminine, singular or plural:

• *de + le* changes to *du*
• *de + les* changes to *des*
• *de + la* and *de + l'* do not change.

Je joue du piano.   I play / am playing the piano.
Elle joue des percussions.   She plays / is playing percussion.
Il joue de la guitare.   He plays / is playing the guitar.

To ask a friend what instrument they play, say:
Tu joues de quel instrument?   What instrument do you play / are you playing?

Or if it's clear you are talking about music, just say:
Tu joues de quoi?   What do you play / are you playing?

Pronunciation

Many of the words for musical instruments are the same or similar to the English words, but be careful! They are often pronounced differently. Listen carefully to the pronunciation in the listening exercises.

 Draw lines to link the pictures to the French words.

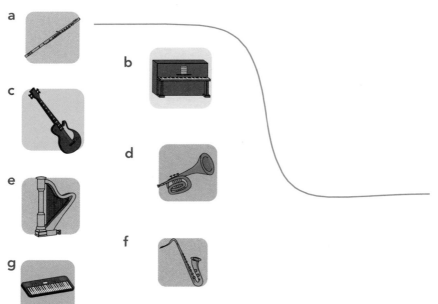

1   le piano

2   la trompette

3   la guitare

4   le clavier

5   la flûte

6   le saxophone

7   la harpe

8   les percussions

2

a Which two French words for instruments in exercise 1 are exactly the same as the English words?

b Which four are very similar to the English words?

c Which word is completely different?

d Why do you think the word *percussions* is plural in French?

3

Write in *du, de la* or *des*.

a Je joue ____du____ violon.

b Louise joue _____ guitare.

c Sarah joue _____ percussions.

d Ethan joue _____ saxophone.

e Clément joue _____ harpe.

f Sofia joue _____ piano.

g Ibrahim joue _____ clavier.

h Yousef joue _____ flûte.

4

Circle the correct words.

a Je joue (au) / du golf.

b Mon ami joue du / au rugby.

c Marc joue à la / de la guitare.

d Christelle joue de la / à la pétanque.

e Nous jouons au / du basket.

f Elle joue au / du violon.

g Quentin joue au / du tennis.

h Margot joue à la / de la trompette.

5

Explain how you chose your answers in exercise 4.

_____

_____

6 In pairs. B chooses an instrument and writes it down. A asks questions to find out what instrument B plays. When A has guessed it, swap roles.

A Tu joues du piano?

B Non! / Oui, je joue du piano.

7 Read the interview. True or false? Write T or F. ⭐

magazine musique   avril edition

TROIS
questions
   à **MARIELLE**

Quelle est ta musique préférée?

Moi, j'adore le R&B, c'est génial! J'aime chanter. J'aime beaucoup Beyoncé, elle est excellente. Je voudrais chanter comme Beyoncé!

Qu'est-ce que tu n'aimes pas comme musique?

Bof, je déteste la musique classique. C'est vraiment nul!

Tu joues d'un instrument de musique?

Non, je chante seulement. Mon frère joue des percussions et moi, je voudrais jouer de la guitare, mais c'est très difficile.

a Marielle is a singer. _____T_____

b She's a fan of classical music. _____

c She sings better than Beyoncé. _____

d She likes R&B. _____

e She plays percussion. _____

f She plays the guitar. _____

g She'd like to play the guitar. _____

h Playing the guitar is easy. _____

8 Write your own answers to these questions in French. In your answer to part **a**, include *j'écoute…, j'adore…, j'aime…* and *je déteste…* ⭐

a Tu écoutes quel genre de musique?

b Tu joues d'un instrument de musique?

• Pupil Book pages 106–107

Aujourd'hui, c'est le _____ . Il est _____ .

Langue et grammaire

Adjectives

Remember that French adjectives change depending on the noun they describe. Usually, you add an 'e' for feminine nouns and an 's' for plural nouns:

un tee-shirt bleu	a blue tee-shirt
des tee-shirts bleus	blue tee-shirts
une chaussure bleue	a blue shoe
des chaussures bleues	blue shoes

When the adjective already ends in 'e', there is no need to add a second:

une jupe jaune	a yellow skirt

Some adjectives are irregular:

	ms	mpl	fs	fpl
beautiful	*beau*	*beaux*	*belle*	*belles*
white	*blanc*	*blancs*	*blanche*	*blanches*

Pouvoir + infinitive

Pouvoir means 'to be able to'. You met the phrase *on peut* (we can) in Module 3. Here are some more forms of this verb:

je peux	I can	*il/elle peut*	he/she can
tu peux	you can	*on peut*	we can

You can follow any of these phrases with a verb in its infinitive form (how it's written in the dictionary):

Je peux aller au parc.   I can go to the park.

Mettre

Mettre means 'to put on' or 'to wear':

je mets	I put on / wear
tu mets	you put on / wear
il/elle met	he/she puts on / wears
on met	we put on / wear

---

1 **Write in the words for the items of clothing.**

short   manteau   pull   jupe   robe   ~~pantalon~~   chemise   veste

a Le ___pantalon___ coûte 30€.

b La _____ coûte 55€.

c La _____ coûte 18€.

d Le _____ coûte 25€.

e La _____ coûte 22€.

f La _____ coûte 53€.

g Le _____ coûte 70€.

h Le _____ coûte 19€.

2 Circle the correct adjective.

a un tee-shirt (gris) / grise

b des chaussettes verts / vertes

c une beau / belle robe

d une chemise blanche / blanc

e une jupe noire / noir

f des chaussures noires / noirs

g un sweat bleu / bleue

h un manteau marrons / marron

3 In pairs. B thinks of an item of clothing and a colour and writes them down. A asks questions to find out what they are. When A has guessed, swap roles.

A C'est une veste jaune?

B Non!

4 Write in the correct form of *mettre*.

a Alain __met__ un tee-shirt noir.

b Qu'est-ce que tu _____ ce soir?

c Je _____ un beau pantalon.

d Linda _____ un jean.

e Qu'est-ce qu'on _____ pour la fête?

f Il _____ une veste blanche.

5 Write the feminine forms of these adjectives.

Masculine	Feminine
a vert	verte
b rouge	_____
c moche	_____
d beau	_____
e bleu	_____
f blanc	_____
g jaune	_____
h gris	_____

6 Think of five items of clothing you'd like to buy. Write a shopping list. Include colours. ⭐

Je voudrais _____

_____

_____

_____

_____

7 Read the article. Work out what the expressions below are in French. ⭐

TROYES

Troyes, dans l'est de la France, est une ville de mode. Ici il ya a des usines qui fabriquent des vêtements pour tout le monde. Les vêtements de sport sont très populaires. Les ados aiment beaucoup les jeans et les baskets. À Troyes il y a beaucoup de «magasins d'usine». On peut y acheter des vêtements de mode à des prix très raisonnables.

a factory _____

b manufacture _____

c trainers _____

d factory outlets _____

e buy _____

f very reasonable prices _____

8 Answer these questions about the article. ⭐

a Where is Troyes? In the _____ of France _____

b What is it famous for? _____

c What can you find there? _____

d What is particularly popular? _____

e What's the advantage of shopping in a *magasin d'usine*? _____

• Pupil Book pages 108–109

Aujourd'hui, c'est le _____ . Il est _____ .

Langue et grammaire

To describe a scene or a situation, use the phrase *il y a*, meaning 'there is' or 'there are'.
Il y a stays the same whether you are describing one thing or several things.

Il y a un pont.	There is a bridge.
Il y a deux filles.	There are two girls.

You can vary your descriptions by using *on voit* from the verb *voir*, which means 'to see'.

On voit un pont.	We can see a bridge.

To say where something is, use phrases such as:

à gauche	on the left
à droite	on the right
au milieu	in the middle
devant	in front
derrière	behind

Remember to use *je pense que* or *à mon avis* to express your opinion.

Je pense que c'est un beau tableau.	I think it's a beautiful painting.
À mon avis c'est un beau tableau.	In my opinion it's a beautiful painting.

 1 Write in the words for the parts of the body.

jambes   pieds   oreille   bouche   ~~tête~~   bras   main   nez

head *la tête*

nose *le _____*

ear *l'_____*

mouth *la _____*

arm *le _____*

hand *la_____*

legs *les _____*

feet *les _____*

2 Solve these anagrams to find the parts of the body.

a nami _____

b zen _____

c sarb _____

d chebou _____

e ettê _____

f rilolee _____

g asejbm _____

h speid _____

3 Copy the words under the correct pictures.

| derrière | devant | au milieu | à gauche | à droite |

a   **b**   **c**   **d**   **e**

_____ _____ _____ _____ _____

4 In pairs. A mimes an expression from exercise 3. B says it in French. Then swap roles.

5 Write in *il y a* or *on voit*.

a __On voit__ un garçon dans le tableau. (We see)

b _____ une chaise devant le lit. (There is)

c _____ des chapeaux verts. (We see)

d _____ une rue avec un pont. (There is)

e _____ deux jambes et deux bras. (We see)

f _____ une table dans la salle à manger. (There is)

6 Translate the sentences in exercise 5 into English.

a _____

b _____

c _____

d _____

e _____

f _____

g _____

h _____

7 Draw a picture based on this description. ⭐

Au milieu, il y a une maison. Derrière la maison, on voit de l'herbe verte. Devant la maison, il y a une rue. À gauche, on voit un garçon. Il porte un chapeau rouge. À droite, il y a un pont.

 8 Translate this description into French. ⭐

In the middle there is a street. There is a cathedral and a bridge. We can see the sky.

_____

_____

• Pupil Book pages 110–111

Aujourd'hui, c'est le _____ . Il est _____ .

Langue et grammaire

Possessives

You already know how to say 'my' in French: *mon*, *ma* or *mes*. Similarly, the French for 'your' can be either *ton*, *ta* or *tes*.

There is no difference in French between 'his' and 'her'. What is important is the word being described. Study the pattern in the table below.

my	**your**	**his/her**
mon frère	*ton frère*	*son frère*
my brother	your brother	his/her brother
ma sœur	*ta sœur*	*sa sœur*
my sister	your sister	his/her sister
mes parents	*tes parents*	*ses parents*
my parents	your parents	his/her parents

Pouvoir and *vouloir*

You already know that the French for 'I can' is *je peux* from the verb *pouvoir*. You can use it to ask for permission:

Je peux regarder un film?   Can I watch a film?

The French for 'I want' is *je veux* from the verb *vouloir*. It follows a similar pattern:

Si tu veux.   If you like.
Qu'est-ce qu'il veut faire?   What does he want to do?

Pronunciation

Notice, also, the way these verbs are pronounced. The letters *eu* are used a lot in French, so be sure to say them correctly.

 1 Fill in the gaps with *son*, *sa* or *ses*.

Voici Oola. Sa sœur s'appelle Soli et _____

frère s'appelle Tota. _____ père est Libi et

_____ mère est Jalo. Alors, _____

parents sont Libi et Jalo. _____ chien

s'appelle Wala.

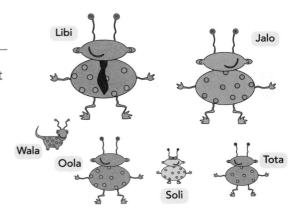

 2 Fill in the gaps with *ton*, *ta*, *tes* or *mon*, *ma*, *mes*.

a Comment s'appelle __ton père__ , Oola?

_____ père s'appelle Libi.

b Comment s'appellent _____ parents?

_____ parents s'appellent Libi et Jalo.

c Comment s'appelle _____ chien?

_____ chien s'appelle Wala.

d Comment s'appelle _____ frère?

_____ frère s'appelle Tota.

e Comment s'appelle _____ sœur?

_____ sœur s'appelle Soli.

3

a In pairs. Ask your partner about his or her family. Then answer your partner's questions. If you haven't got any brothers and sisters, just invent some!

A Comment s'appelle ton frère?

B Mon frère s'appelle…

b Tell someone else what you have found out about your partner.

A Son frère s'appelle…

 4   Draw lines to link the English and French expressions.

his dog	ta maison
her friend	avec moi
your house	si tu veux
I want	on peut
your parents	son copain
with you	je veux
with me	son chien
if you want	avec toi
he wants	tes parents
we can	il veut

 5   Say that you want to do these things using *Je veux*…

regarder la télé	écouter de la musique	regarder un film	jouer au tennis
faire ses devoirs	faire une balade	aller en ville	aller au lit
nager dans la mer	faire la vaisselle	faire de l'équitation	manger un gâteau

a watch a film   *Je veux regarder un film.*

b play tennis   _____

c go to bed   _____

d eat a cake   _____

e swim in the sea   _____

f do the washing up   _____

6 Give permission to do these things using *Tu peux...*

  a listen to music   Tu peux écouter de la musique.

  b watch TV   _____

  c go into town   _____

  d go for a walk   _____

  e go horse riding   _____

  f do your homework   _____

7 Read the text and answer the questions in English. ⭐

> Aujourd'hui, c'est samedi. Je veux aller en ville, regarder un film et manger au restaurant. Mais je ne peux pas, parce que je n'ai pas d'argent. Mes parents disent, «Tu ne peux pas aller en ville. Tu peux rester à la maison, faire tes devoirs et aller au lit. C'est tout.» Je ne suis pas contente!

  a What things does Sophie want to do?

  _____

  b Why can't she do them?

  _____

  c What things **can** she do?

  _____

  d How does she feel about it?

  _____

8 **a** Write down, in French, three things you **want** to do. Try to use expressions you learned in earlier modules and topics. ⭐

  Je veux _____

  _____

  b Write three things you **can** do.

  Je peux _____

  _____

• Pupil Book pages 112–113

Aujourd'hui, c'est le _____ . Il est _____ .

Langue et grammaire

The perfect tense

To talk about something you saw or did in the past, you use a past tense. One of the most commonly used in French is called the perfect tense. To make the perfect tense, you use the present tense of *avoir* followed by a form of the verb you need to use called the past participle.

To make the past participle of *–er* verbs, remove the *–er* ending and replace it with é.

infinitive	past participle	past perfect tense
regarder	*regardé*	*j'ai regardé*
aimer	*aimé*	*j'ai aimé*

If you want to use the negative form, place *ne ... pas* around the part of the verb *avoir*:

je n'ai pas aimé   I didn't like   *je n'ai pas regardé*   I didn't watch

Some irregular verbs have different forms of past participles.

infinitive	past participle	past perfect tense
faire	*fait*	*j'ai fait*
voir	*vu*	*j'ai vu*

Once you know the past participle, you can follow the same rule with *tu, il, elle* and *on*.

tu as aimé   you liked   *il/elle/on a aimé*   he/she/we liked

 1 Write in the past participles of these *–er* verbs.

aimer	_____aimé_____	écouter	_____
regarder	_____	manger	_____
adorer	_____	trouver	_____
acheter	_____	admirer	_____

 2 In the box you will find various parts of verbs. Copy them into the correct columns.

je regarde	manger	j'aime	voir	je fais
je mange	faire	aimé	fait	je vois
regarder	mangé	regardé	vu	aimer

	Infinitive	Present tense	Past participle
watch	regarder		
like			
see			
eat			
do			

3 Insert the correct past participle.

écouté   aimé   regardé   trouvé   visité   vu   mangé   acheté

a J'ai ____visité____ la Tour Eiffel. (visited)

b J'ai _____ les bâtiments de Paris. (saw)

c J'ai _____ dans un restaurant au premier étage. (ate)

d J'ai _____ des souvenirs. (bought)

e J'ai _____ les touristes. (watched)

f J'ai _____ beaucoup de conversations. (listened to)

g J'ai _____ l'ambiance. (liked)

h J'ai _____ tout ça excellent. (found)

4 Unjumble these sentences in the perfect tense, which describe a day at the Centre Pompidou.

a aimé Pompidou J'ai Centre le

    J'ai aimé le Centre Pompidou.

b tableau a On un vu Picasso de

    _____

c sur vue regardé la J'ai Paris

    _____

d café a du On le mangé dans Centre

    _____

e moderne J'ai l'art adoré

    _____

f trouvé J'ai intéressant Centre le très

    _____

5 In pairs. A makes up sentences using *manger, regarder* and *faire* in the present tense. B is a know-it-all and says they've already done whatever A says! Then swap roles.

A J'écoute la radio.

B J'ai *déjà* écouté la radio.

déjà = already

6 Read the text. Answer the questions with 'yes' or 'no'.

J'ai aimé le Centre Pompidou mais je n'ai pas aimé le musée d'Orsay.

J'ai regardé Astérix mais je n'ai pas regardé Tintin.

J'ai mangé une pizza mais je n'ai pas mangé de nouilles.

J'ai fait les courses mais je n'ai pas fait mes devoirs.

J'ai vu Star Wars mais je n'ai pas vu Star Trek.

a Did Patricia like the Musée d'Orsay?
No

b Did she eat a pizza?
____

c Did she do the shopping?
____

d Did she see Star Trek?
____

e Did she do her homework?
____

f Did she eat noodles?
____

g Did she watch Tintin?
____

h Did she watch Astérix?
____

i Did she see Star Wars?
____

j Did she like the Centre Pompidou?
____

 7 Translate this paragraph into English. ⭐

Lundi, j'ai visité le musée d'art moderne à Rouen. J'ai vu les tableaux et j'ai aimé les sculptures. J'ai mangé du gâteau au café-bar et mon copain Roger a acheté des souvenirs.

_____

_____

_____

 8 Describe a holiday or an outing you went on last year. Write a sentence about: ⭐

- something you saw
- something you ate
- something you heard
- something you did
- something you liked
- something you didn't like.

Topic 6 La fête de la musique

• Pupil Book pages 114–115

Aujourd'hui, c'est le _____ . Il est _____ .

Langue et grammaire

The perfect tense with *être*

In the previous topic, you learnt how to use the present tense of *avoir* followed by a past participle to say what you did in the past using the perfect tense.

Some common verbs, such as *aller* and *rester*, use the present tense of *être* instead of *avoir* to make the perfect tense. The past participle is formed in the same way.

je suis allé(e)	I went
tu es allé(e)	you went
il est allé	he went
elle est allée	she went
on est allé(e)(s)	we went

Note that you need to add an extra *e* at the end of the past participle if the action is performed by a girl or a woman.

Ma sœur est allée au concert, mon frère est resté à la maison.

My sister went to the concert, my brother stayed at home.

Making suggestions

When discussing what to do with friends, use *je voudrais* plus an infinitive to introduce what you would like to do, or *on pourrait* to make a suggestion of what you could do.

Je voudrais aller…	I would like to go…
On pourrait regarder…	We could watch…

 1 Complete the sentences below using *suis, es* or *est.*

a Je __suis__ allé en ville.   __M__

b Tu _____ allée au concert?   _____

c Il _____ allé au collège.   _____

d On _____ allés en France.   _____

e Elle _____ allée au restaurant.   _____

f Je _____ restée à la maison.   _____

g Il _____ resté dans la cuisine.   _____

h Tu _____ restée longtemps.   _____

i Elle _____ restée au lit.   _____

j On _____ restés cinq minutes.   _____

 2 Next to each sentence in exercise 1, write 'F' if it refers to a female, 'M' if it refers to a male and 'G' if it refers to a group.

3 Translate these sentences into English.

a Je suis resté. _____I stayed._____

b Elle est allée. _____

c Il est sorti. _____

d Tu es restée. _____

e On est allés. _____

f Je suis allé. _____

4 In pairs. A says where they'd like to go, using *Je voudrais aller*... B replies with suggestions, using *On pourrait aller*... Then swap roles.

5 Translate these sentences into French.

a A boy saying 'I stayed'. _____Je suis resté._____

b A girl saying 'I stayed'. _____

c A boy saying 'I went'. _____

d A girl saying 'I went'. _____

e He stayed. _____

f She stayed. _____

g He went. _____

h She went. _____

6 Circle the correct verb.

a Il **est** / a resté à la maison.

b Je **suis** / J'ai joué de la musique.

c On a / **est** allés à un concert.

d Ma sœur **est** / a restée dans sa chambre.

e Mon oncle a / **est** mangé une pomme.

f Tu **as** / es allé au musée?

Read Yasmine's email and answer the questions in English. ⭐

À: Lena

Salut Lena,
Je pense à notre week-end à Paris. Qu'est-ce qu'on pourrait faire? Moi, je voudrais aller au musée d'Orsay,
parce que j'adore l'art. Mais je n'aime pas l'art moderne, alors je ne voudrais pas aller au Centre Pompidou.
On pourrait faire du shopping aux Champs-Elysées et visiter l'Arc de Triomphe. C'est une bonne idée? Le soir,
on pourrait manger des tajines dans un restaurant marocain. Je ne voudrais pas manger dans une pizzeria
parce que je n'aime pas le fromage.
À bientôt!
Yasmine

---

a One thing she would like to do.

_____

b Two things she wouldn't like to do.

_____

_____

c Two reasons she gives for her preferences.

_____

_____

d Three things she suggests they could do.

_____

_____

_____

8 **Write an email like Yasmine's in exercise 7. Choose a different city and different things to do. Use _je voudrais…, je ne veux pas…_ and on _pourrait…_** ⭐

_____

_____

_____

Notes